The American Exploration and Travel Series

(Complete list on page 168)

The Snake Country Expedition of 1830–1831

The Snake Country
EXPEDITION
of 1830-1831

John Work's Field Journal

Edited by

FRANCIS D. HAINES, JR.

UNIVERSITY OF OKLAHOMA PRESS : NORMAN

By Francis D. Haines, Jr.

Gold on Sterling Creek (with Vern S. Smith) (Medford, Oregon, 1964)

Jacksonville: Biography of a Gold Camp (Medford, Oregon, 1967)

A Bride on the Bozeman Trail, by Ellen Gordon Fletcher (editor) (Medford, Oregon, 1970)

The Snake Country Expedition of 1830–1831: John Work's Field Journal, (editor) (Norman, Oklahoma, 1971)

International Standard Book Number: 0-8061-0947-5.

Library of Congress Catalog Card Number: 70-145501.

The Snake Country Expedition of 1830–31; John Work's Field Journal is Volume 59 in *The American Exploration and Travel Series.*

For Leslie, in hopes that this
will exorcise the ghost of
John Work

Acknowledgments

Permission to publish this journal has been granted by Mr. Willard Ireland, Archivist and Librarian, Provincial Archives, Victoria, British Columbia. Mr. Ireland and his staff were also most generous in making available the materials in the Archives that were useful in editing this work.

The following persons made major contributions to the editing of this journal: Father William L. Davis, S. J., Gonzaga University; Francis Haines, Monmouth, Oregon; Miss A. M. Johnson, Hudson's Bay Company Archives, London; Miss Priscilla Knuth, Oregon Historical Society, Portland, Oregon; Professor David E. Miller, University of Utah, Salt Lake City, Utah; and Mr. Merle Wells, Idaho State Historical Society, Boise, Idaho.

A host of others, too many to mention by name, have also made contributions to the editing. I take this opportunity of expressing again my thanks to them for their assistance. The editor assumes full responsibility for the use which has been made of each contribution.

Perhaps my greatest debt is to my family. Its contribution to this work entitles each member to credit on the title page.

FRANCIS D. HAINES, JR.

Ashland, Oregon
January, 1971

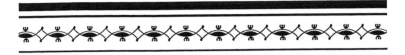

Contents

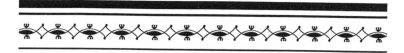

Illustrations

Map

Editor's Introduction

The history of the Pacific Northwest really begins with the third voyage of Captain James Cook, 1776–78. The discovery, by Cook's sailors, that furs acquired on the Northwest coast commanded a ready market in China led a number of British and American merchants into the maritime fur trade. It was a discovery that was particularly important to the Western world as it had had great difficulty in finding goods which the Chinese would accept in trade.

The resulting rush to the Northwest coast culminated in the Nootka Sound incident in 1788. In the settlement which ended the dispute, Spain relinquished its claims to exclusive right to the Northwest coast above forty-two degrees north latitude. The agreement, between Spain and Britain, also stated that the principle of actual occupation of the territory north of forty-two degrees would determine its eventual disposition.

The British were soon forced to withdraw from the maritime trade as the wars resulting from the French Revolution increased in scope. This withdrawal left the area open to exploitation by American merchants, who were eager to replace the markets in the British Empire which had largely been lost to them as the result of the war for independence.

The maritime fur trade became less economical as time passed. The Chinese market became saturated with furs except for the comparatively rare pelt of the sea otter, which had always commanded premium prices. By 1805, American vessels were reduced to serving as common carriers in the Indian economy of the Northwest coast, trading small cargoes of fish oil and slaves between coastal villages as their captains attempted, with little success, to acquire furs suitable for the Chinese market.

It was not until 1810 that permanent occupation of the region began. John Jacob Astor, a leading American fur trader, organized his Pacific Fur Company to establish permanent trading posts in the Northwest to tap the interior and to take over the time-consuming duty of collecting a cargo, which was making the maritime trade so unprofitable. At the same time, the Northwest Company, a Canadian firm based in Montreal, was establishing posts west of the Rocky Mountains, hoping to tap the rich trapping area west of the mountains and to reach the Pacific coast to take advantage of the low cost of transport by sea which would replace the thousand-mile supply line from Montreal that depended on canoes.

The failure of the Astor venture and the eventual sale of its assets to the Northwest Company in 1813 left the United States with no permanent settlements in the region. It appeared that the Northwest would be left to the British. The bright dream of spanning the continent, which had received such impetus from the Louisiana Purchase of 1803, seemed to be shattered.

The United States was, however, unwilling to give up. It negotiated with Britain on the subject of the Pacific Northwest, but without success. In 1818 the two nations finally agreed to a treaty of Joint Occupation, which was to run for ten years and which, essentially, was a postponement of the solution. The ten-year period passed with no change in the diplomatic position, and the treaty was renewed for an indefinite period in 1827.

The American westward movement was land borne, and the British move to the Pacific Northwest was also an overland movement. The key to control of the region was the great Columbia River system. Since the drainage of the Snake River was the most accessible portion of the Pacific Northwest to American overland travelers, control of the Snake River country was essential to the struggle for empire. Crucial was that part of the Snake River which stretched from the Continental Divide to Hells Canyon, the Snake Country. British defense of the region hinged on control of the Snake Country.

The British effort was taken over in 1821 by the Hudson's Bay Company as the result of the royally ordered merger of that firm with the Northwest Company. From 1824, the year of Governor George Simpson's reorganization of the Columbia Department, until the boundary settlement in 1846, Hudson's Bay Company waged a vigorous battle for control of the Northwest.

The primary tool of the Hudson's Bay Company in this battle was the Snake Country expedition. Its mission was to turn the Snake Country into a fur-trapping desert. Long before Frederick Jackson Turner had evolved his frontier thesis or Ellen Semple had produced her dichotomy of trap versus plow, the governor and committee of the Hudson's Bay Company had recognized the American frontier progression of fur trapper, fur trade post, and permanent settler. By rendering the area economically unattractive to the American trapper, the governor and committee hoped to arrest the progression.

The tool selected, the Snake Country expedition, lay at hand, but the company's use of the tool was the first purposeful employment of the brigade. At the time of Governor Simpson's 1824 visit to the Columbia Department, the brigade consisted largely of Iroquois, who trapped in the summer and spent the winter roistering at Spokane House or following one of the Indian tribes.

Trapping the Snake Country had begun with the party led by John Reed of the overland Astorians in 1813. Building huts near the present site of Boise, Idaho, the party began trapping, but was soon wiped out by the Indians, probably the Bannocks. The only survivors were the fabulous Madame Dorion and her two children.

Donald McKenzie, an American, managed to obtain permission from the inert, inefficient management of the Astoria concern to trap the Snake Country and spent the winter of 1813 near Lewiston, Idaho, on the Snake River. Later he was to penetrate the middle Snake River area and make the hazardous boat trip through Hells Canyon, a feat that even the energetic McKenzie did not care to repeat.

From this beginning, the Snake Country expeditions grew to a large band of trappers who wandered through what is now southern and central Idaho. After McKenzie left the service of the Northwest Company, the leadership descended upon other, less capable men. By 1823 even the vigorous leadership of Finan MacDonald was unable to accomplish much with the Iroquois trappers who made up the majority of the party.

The expedition received new life and direction as the result of Governor Simpson's visit in 1824. Peter Skene Ogden was placed in charge, the party was given orders to conduct a winter hunt, and Ogden was ordered to explore the country thoroughly and to trap it out.

Ogden completed this difficult assignment in the period from 1824 to 1830. After almost all of his Iroquois deserted him for the American service in the winter of 1825, Ogden led a brigade composed largely of French-Canadians and "natives" (the company term for half-bloods) through the entire Snake Country, a term which was now enlarged to include the Humboldt drainage, a river which Ogden discovered. Ogden explored as far south as the Colorado River in Arizona with the group which he led back to Fort Nez Perces in June, 1830.

There he learned that he was to turn over the command of the brigade to John Work, his companion on the canoe voyage from York Factory to Fort George (Astoria) when the two came to the Columbia Department in 1823. Work was to lead the party on its 1830–31 expedition. It is Work's field journal of that expedition which follows.

Exploring was no longer a mission of the Snake Country expedition. Ogden had left little to explore. His directions to Work (see Appendix B) directed the new leader to the areas which had, previously, yielded the richest harvests of pelts. The major task of the party was to be the trapping out of the Snake Country.

Work discovered that, although the Snake Country was not trapped out in an absolute sense, it would no longer yield sufficient furs to support a brigade. On his return from the 1830–31 expedition, he reported this finding to John McLoughlin.

By that time it was too late to deploy the party elsewhere for the coming season. McLoughlin, on Work's recommendation, directed him to trap the Salmon River and cross the mountains to trap in the Flathead country. The area had been touched by earlier Snake Country expeditions, but the difficulty of the terrain and the aggressions of the Blackfeet turned the year into a horrible ordeal for the parties and they had left it alone. The brigade of 1831–32 was to experience all of these difficulties in full measure, starving at times, having men drowned in the Salmon River, and losing others to the Blackfeet. Furthermore, the returns in furs were not great.

The brigade was sent to California for the season of 1832–33. Influenza plagued the party through the entire year. At the conclusion of that expedition, Work was reassigned and the personnel of the brigade were distributed through the Columbia Department.

The Snake Country, however, was still the object of Hudson's Bay Company attention. Fort Boise was established in 1835 to provide a center for the Indian trade, and Fort Hall was purchased from New Englander Nathaniel Wyeth. A small party spent the summers trading with the Indians until the tide of immigration began sweeping through the Snake Country in 1843.

Hudson's Bay Company policy had been well conceived and well executed. American trappers were turned back at the edge of the Snake Country and soon left it, but the scarcity of beaver did not prevent American settlers from entering the region. The mission movement, which began in the Willamette Valley with the Jason Lee group of 1834 and at Lapwai and Waiilatpu under Henry Harmon Spalding and Marcus Whitman, played an important role in enticing waves of settlers to the region in the 1840's. It was the immigration of the 1840's that was to sweep the Pacific Northwest, south of forty-nine degrees north latitude, into the United States.

The route of the brigades into the Snake Country became the Oregon Trail of the immigrants. The Snake Country brigades had won the battle with the American fur traders, but Hudson's Bay Company had lost the war.

JOHN WORK

John Work was born about 1792 at Geroddy Farm near South Johnstown, County Donegal. He was the eldest of the six children of Henry Wark. We know nothing of the early life of John Work. It can be assumed that he was given a good education on the basis of his hand, his rhetoric, and the extent of his vocabulary as evidenced by his journals and letters.

He joined the Hudson's Bay Company on June 15, 1814, at Stromness in the Orkney Islands. At that time he anglicized his surname to Work. At twenty-two years of age he was embarked on the career that was to occupy the remainder of his life.

Work's first few years in the Hudson's Bay Company service were spent at or in the vicinity of Hudson's Bay. He began as a post steward and worked his way up to the commissioned rank of clerk. This period was his apprenticeship in the fur trade.

John Work was assigned to the Columbia Department in 1823. He was among the first wave of new men sent to this farthest reach of company operations by Governor George Simpson. The Columbia Department had become a part of Hudson's Bay Company in March, 1821, by the merger with the Northwest Company. By the summer of 1823 the governor and committee had resolved to re-organize the Department completely or to abandon it. Work was one of those sent in to become acquainted with the region and to be available for Simpson's visit of 1824.

Work left York Factory, the headquarters of company operations in North America, on July 18, 1823. He and Peter Skene Ogden were bound for the Columbia Department with the latter in charge of the trip. Simpson chose well, for both young men were to carve for themselves important niches in the history of the Northwest.

Work's first assignment in the Columbia Department was Spokane House. He spent his first winter in the region as one of the clerks in this post which was the center of the fur trade in the Columbia Basin region. The following year found Work on duty at Fort George on the lower Columbia River, headquarters of the Columbia Department. In 1825 he returned to Spokane House with orders to begin construction of a new post at Kettle Falls which would replace the awkwardly located Northwest Company post on the Little Spokane River.

Work's experiences during these years were varied. Twice he had the company of the young botanist David Douglas on trips in the field. On two other occasions he drove herds of horses across country, the latter being the difficult drive from Kettle Falls to Fort Vancouver.

It was during this period that Work married, in the "mountain fashion," Josette Legacé, a Spokane Indian woman. Josette was to share the remainder of his life and to bear him eleven children. There is little mention of her in the journals, but Work was devoted to her and, on November 6, 1849, married her in a formal ceremony at Victoria, British Columbia.

In 1830, Peter Skene Ogden was relieved of command of the Snake Country expedition to work more closely with John McLoughlin in the administration of the Columbia Department. This change opened the way to Work's appointment to his first major command. That this step came as a result of appreciation of his services is proved by his promotion to the rank of chief trader long before the governor and committee in London could have made any decision on his effectiveness in the new post. The commission was dated November 3, 1830, while Work was leading his party on the Pahsimeroi River in eastern Idaho.

On his return from the Snake Country in July, 1830, Work reported to Dr. John McLoughlin at Fort Vancouver. It was obvious that the Snake Country would no longer support a brigade. Unable, at such short notice, to employ the brigade in some other region or to disperse its personnel to other assignments, McLoughlin accepted Work's suggestion and ordered the party to hunt the Salmon River and cross the mountains to the eastward to hunt the Clark Fork and its tributaries in what is now western Montana.

The rugged terrain and the predatory Blackfeet both took a serious toll of the men and horses of the party. The brigade that Work led back to Fort Vancouver in 1832 was in poor condition, but its troubles were not over. Influenza, which had been introduced on the lower Columbia, probably by the ship *Isabelle*, struck the brigade with a vengeance.

McLoughlin had decided to employ the brigade in the Central Valley of California. A small party of trappers, under the leadership of Michel Laframboise, had been working northern California. McLoughlin intended to send that party down the coast and send the Snake Country brigade into the interior valleys.

The expedition to Bonaventura of 1832–33 was another ordeal for John Work. Fever racked the men, women, and children of the party throughout the trip. On one occasion Work reported that there was not a single person in camp able to get to his feet.

John Work was a long time recovering from his illness and its aftereffects. He spent the winter of 1833–34 at Fort Vancouver as an invalid. Following his recovery in the spring, he made two small field trips.

Work spent most of the year of 1835 engaged in the coasting trade north toward Alaska. He was in charge of the voyage, a position that required some diplomacy and some forthright firmness in dealing with the captains of the vessels.

In January, 1836, Work was assigned to Fort Simpson on the British Columbia coast. The climate made it one of the most wretched of the company posts to serve. He was assigned command of the trade at the fort and along the coast but his authority was not clear cut. It was a trying position, and his ten years at Fort Simpson embittered him. Work's position improved in 1846 when he was finally promoted to the rank of chief factor and given full command of Fort Simpson and the coastal trade.

In 1849, Work was joined with James Douglas and Peter Skene Ogden on the board which governed company operations in the northwest region. He remained at Fort Simpson until 1852, but his new duties permitted him to travel, thus giving him brief respites from the rigors of life at the unpleasant post.

On leaving Fort Simpson, Work moved with his family to Vancouver Island. The three-man board, headquartered at Fort Victoria, occupied his time and his attention. He was to remain there as a member of the board until his death.

Work began purchasing land on Vancouver Island and continued until he had amassed a total of a little more than thirteen hundred acres, which made him the largest landowner on the island. Some of the land was developed for agriculture, and Work seems to have made the venture quite profitable.

John Work's last years were full. He became a member of the appointed Legislative Council for the island in 1853 and held the post until his death. Although company operations declined in scope, there was much to be done in directing the variety of activities and in pressing the land claims of the Hudson's Bay Company.

Work's personal life was a mixture of satisfactions and disappointments. He lived to see five of his eight daughters happily married. His two surviving sons were a sore disappointment to him, both earning bad reputations in the community.

The rigors of his long life in the field levied their toll. In his sixty-ninth year he was forced to his bed where he lingered for two months. On December 22, 1861, he died in Victoria. His faithful Josette was to survive him by thirty-four years.

Work's personality is difficult to assess. The descriptions in detail that make his journals so valuable tend to hide his personality. He seems to have been quiet and stiff in relationships with others except for his few very close friends. Governor Simpson characterized him as a man without friends and disliked by his colleagues. As usual with the governor's assessments, this seems to have been an exaggeration with a foundation in fact.

Work was a conscientious man and meticulous in his performance of duty. His assiduous attention to minutiae must have made him a somewhat trying colleague. It was a characteristic he shared with Sir James Douglas, but Work lacked the administrative skill and the learning of his Scottish colleague. He also lacked the irritating conceit of Douglas.

John Work's career spanned most of the period of the land fur trade in the Pacific Northwest. He lived to see the primitive regions he had traveled in pursuit of pelts become settled and some of the areas subjected to the ravages of the gold rush.

Much of what we know of the day-to-day operation of the Hudson's Bay Company in the Northwest is learned from Work's journals. His contribution is more than in the mere existence of the journals. His powers of description and the detail of his accounts create vivid images of this colorful era. Only the figures of Dr. John McLoughlin and Peter Skene Ogden stand out more brilliantly in the history of the fur trade in the Northwest.

EDITOR'S NOTE

Hudson's Bay Company required that reports be filed from each post concerning the Indians of the vicinity, the flora, the fauna, the soil, and the climate. Additional information was frequently requested through questionnaires circulated to post commanders. Most of the information was requested in order to facilitate planning and direction of company activities. The governor and committee did, on several occasions, require information in response to requests from scholars and learned societies.

Journals were required of exploring expeditions. This demand explains in part the keeping of journals on the Snake Country expeditions. Another factor was the presence of the American boundary and the joint occupancy of the Northwest. Collisions between company parties and Americans might very well develop into full-scale international incidents. Journals, such as this one, could be valuable evidence in such event.

Reports from the Snake Country were read in London, as Ogden discovered. He headed a letter "headwaters of the Missouri" and received a stinging rebuke from the governor and committee for invading American territory. The amusing side of the incident is that Ogden was not even near American territory on this expedition.

Work seems to have kept a journal on most of his independent commands when traveling. The earliest of these journals is of his trip across the continent to the Pacific Northwest in 1823 (though he was not in charge in this instance). He submitted copies of some of these journals to the governor and committee.

Work retained sixteen of his field journals when he retired from company service. On his death these journals passed to his descendants, who, in turn, gave them to the Provincial Archives of the Province of British Columbia.

That these journals are the actual field journals is beyond doubt. The London copy of the 1830–31 Snake Country journal is a fair hand copy of the field journal and shows some signs of editing. This is most obvious in the entry for September 25, 1830. The field journals are written in a crabbed but legible hand which contrasts sharply with the flowing, legible hand of the London copy and those of Work's letters written when he had a desk or writing table available.

The field journals are written in ink which Work probably carried with him in powdered form and made up as needed. The ink varies greatly in density through the journal.

Part I of this journal was kept in a standard Hudson's Bay Company notebook with the usual company stamps present on the pages. The paper is lined on both sides and Work used both sides of the page. These loose sheets were pierced and tied between leather covers with leather thongs.

The London copy of the journal preserves the division of the field journal. This is a point of interest in that the notebook used for it could easily have contained the entire text.

The journals are well preserved and excellently cared for. There are, however, some fading of the ink and some staining of the pages. To deal with these problems, the editor used a negative microfilm copy of the field journal. The film was especially useful in identifying additions as such and brought out the writing which stains make illegible to the naked eye.

Part I of the field journal has not been previously published. Sketchy notes from the London copy, taken by Agnes Laut, were published by T. C. Elliott in the *Oregon Historical Quarterly*. It does not seem to have occurred to scholars that the field journal might be more complete than this version until Henry Drummond Dee made his study of John Work. Miss Laut apparently did not see Part II of the London journal.

Part II of the field journal was published in 1913 in a version edited by T. C. Elliott for the *Oregon Historical Quarterly*. The transcription provided for Elliott was inaccurate in many places.

In preparing the text for presentation, the original pagination of the journals has not been kept. It is felt that the identification of each entry by date is sufficient.

The editor has attempted to retain as much of the flavor of the original as possible. Typographical considerations prevent the utilization of the dash in punctuation and superscript letters in abbreviations. Unwitting repetitions and tag words have been eliminated. For ease of reading, periods have been substituted for what seem to be commas in some portions of the manuscript.

Interlineations have been italicized. These words and passages are marked in order to give the reader an awareness of the process of composition and, it is hoped, an insight into Work's mind. This device was chosen because of its simplicity.

In identifying the personnel of the brigade, a note has been placed in the text the first time a name appears. A more complete account has been placed in Appendix A, where the men are listed alphabetically by surname.

In tracing the route of the party, an attempt has been made to standardize the references by referring to present-day place names as given in the series of state maps issued by the U.S. Geological Survey (1:500,000). This series has been supplemented when necessary by the most reliable source at hand.

The Snake Country Expedition of 1830–1831

August 22
to September 1, 1830

Augt 1830, Sundy 22. On the 15th Inst the Snake Trappers reached Fort Nezperces from Vancouver with their supplies,[1] the few following days were occupied arranging them with horses &c and on friday the 20th they moved off from the fort. I remained two days after to arrange some papers & Accounts and write some letters, And this morning took leave of Mr Ogden[2] & Mr Barnston[3] at N. P. and in four hours smart riding came up with the camp a short distance from the foot of the Blue Mountains. The distance I came today I reckon 24 to 30

[1] The party had left Fort Vancouver on August 4. The group included Ogden's men of the previous year with some men from the brigade which Alexander Roderick McLeod had led into California. (Burt Brown Barker, ed., *The Letters of Dr. John McLoughlin Written at Fort Vancouver, 1829–1832*, 138. Hereafter cited as Barker, *McLoughlin Letters.*)

[2] Peter Skene Ogden, chief trader, had been in command of the Snake Country expeditions since 1824. He was later promoted to chief factor and was one of the members of the board in charge of the Columbia Department. He is notable in Northwest history for his prompt and courageous rescue of the survivors of the Whitman massacre.

[3] George Barnston, clerk, was in charge of Fort Nez Perces at this time, having succeeded Samuel Black in June, 1830. He continued in command of the post until the following year. He was later promoted to chief factor. (E. E. Rich, ed., *The Letters of John McLoughlin from Fort Vancouver to the Governor and Committee, First Series, 1825–1838*, Vol. IV [1941] of Hudson's Bay Record Society, 227. Hereafter cited as *HBRS*, IV. A biography of Barnston is to be found in E. E. Rich, ed., *Minutes of the Council of the Northern Department of Rupert Land, 1821–1831*, Vol. III [1940] of the Hudson's Bay Record Society, 427.)

Miles E. S. E.[4] The party consists of 38 Men including myself besides a slave & two youths in all 41 Armed and able to bear arms, And 29 women   22 Boys   23 Girls making a total of 115 Souls[5] who have 21 lodges to shelter them from the weather, and 272 horses & *Mules* to transport themselves and baggage, & *perform the hunting duties.* they are at present pretty well laden in part with provisions as the first part of our journey lies through a country in which Animals are scarce. The party have 337 Traps. On nearly arriving at the camp my horse fell with me when I received a severe fall,   None of my bones are broke but I received a severe shock.

Monday 23. Warm sultry weather. Moved on 2 hours march about 8 miles E. S. E. to the foot of the Mountain, the reason for stopping so early was the want of an encampment farther on except at too great a distance. Several of the horses are also lean which renders short days marches absolutely necessary in order that they may not become jaded at the commencement of the journey, which is to last till our return this time twelve month. Both yesterday & today we encamped on branch of the Walla-walla river.[6]

Tuesdy 24. Weather as yesterday. Made an early start and at the end of 5 hours march encamped on a little plain, a little

[4] The camp would have been located on Pine Creek near the present site of Weston, Oregon.

[5] The figure is given as 114 in the London copy of the journal (T. C. Elliott, ed., "Journal of John Work, Covering Snake Country Expedition of 1830–31," *Oregon Historical Quarterly*, Vol. XIII [1912], 365. Hereafter cited as *OHQ.*). I assume that the discrepancy is accounted for in that Work includes himself in the total in the field journal but not in the copy. The copy further breaks down the total as follows: twenty-six Canadians, two Americans, six half bloods from east of the mountains, two Iroquois, and one Nippesing.

[6] Pine Creek. The trail becomes quite steep above here and there is no place adequate for a camp which requires grazing for 272 animals.

to the Eastward of the summit of the Blue Mountain. Our course the same as yesterday, distance 18 to 20 Miles. The forepart of the journey the road lay up a succession of bare hills, afterwards through thick woods, the road though steep and in some places a little stony in general not bad. One of the engaged men[7] lost one of his horses, in quest of which I had to send back a party of men, who have not yet returned. There is good feeding here for the horses. Four Cayouse Indians[8] are going the same road as us to the buffaloe and keep company with us, they have no women with them, but a slave girl belonging to one of them, Young Allicat's[9] brother, followed him & had been sent back, but again came on, and today he on her refusing to return, shot her. she is wounded in three places, but supposed not mortally.

Wedy. 25. It was noon before the men returned with the stray horse and load, when it was too late to move camp today.

Thursday 26. Cloudy but warm weather. Started early and at the end of 7 hours march about 25 miles generally E. S. E. encamped at the foot of the mountain on a small branch of the Grand ronde river at the entrance of the Grand ronde. The road down the mountain lay mostly through thick woods & though several steep hills were to ascend and descend, is generally good. On arrival at the camp all hands were employed getting lodge

[7] The *engagés* were under contract to the company for the year at a fixed salary. On an expedition such as this, they were supplied with horses, food, traps, and ammunition. The proceeds of their traps belonged to the company.

[8] The Cayuse were a small tribe allied with the Nez Percé. Originally of a different linguistic stock, they spoke Shahaptian.

[9] Young Allicat may be the father of the Nez Percé chief, Old Joseph, and, thus, the grandfather of the Chief Joseph of the Nez Percé War of 1877. (Francis Haines, *Red Eagles of the Northwest*, 73. Hereafter cited as *Red Eagles.)*

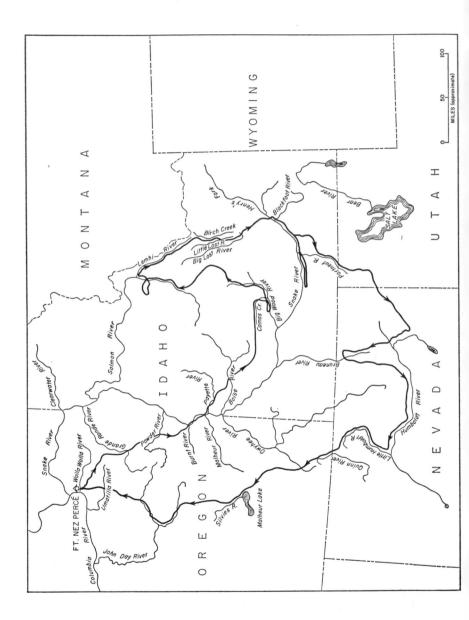

poles as this is the last place where any can be obtained, as the country we are to pass through soon becomes destitute of wood.

Friday 27. Fine weather. Did not move camp today in order to allow all the people time to finish their poles. Some of the young men came ahead of the camp yesterday to hunt, A. Finlay[10] and M. Plant[11] killed a young Elk and a chivereau.[12] Some were out today also but killed nothing, except a few salmon which are found in the river small as it is. Some of the people set some traps for beaver in the evening.

Satdy 28. Fine weather. Moved camp and crossed the grand ronde to the stiff clay fork, $5\frac{1}{2}$ hours march about 22 Miles along the W. side of the river viz. $1\frac{1}{2}$ hours E. S. E. and four hours S. S. W.[13] encamped on the South side of the Fork. Pichette[14] killed 2 small Beaver, which is the commencement of our hunt, the others got nothing. Some salmon were killed in this creek.

Sundy 29. Warm sultry weather. Course S. E. by E 2 hours across the remainder of the grand ronde to the foot of the Mountain. and 1 hour & 40 Minutes same course up the hills and to the fountain[15] where we encamped in all about 12 to 14 miles. Some of the people hunting but killed nothing.

[10] Augustin Finlay. He was probably one of the sons of the noted Jacques Rafael "Jacco" Finlay.

[11] Michel Plante was probably the brother of Antoine Plante, who was also a member of this brigade. His first engagement with the company was in 1828.

[12] French-Canadian for deer. Work usually employed this term in preference to the English.

[13] Mill Creek. The camp would be located between the present communities of Union and La Grande.

[14] Louis Pichette. He had been employed in the Columbia Department as early as 1818.

[15] From the French-Canadian *fontaine*, meaning a spring or the source of a stream. The site would be near Union, Oregon.

Mondy 30. Blowing fresh towards ev[en]ing. Proceeded from the Fountain to Powder river 3½ hours march about 14 Miles S. E. the road good along a fine valley, steep mountains on both sides. Crossed two small branches before reaching the one on which we encamped, this is only a small stream, about 10 yd. wide, and shallow, there are a good many salmon in it. some of the people took a few of them, they are but indifferent but the people relish them well. The people had bad implements for catching them or several more might have been taken. Several of the people set some traps, Depot[16] took three beaver.

Tuesdy 31. Blowing fresh and cool towards evening. Marched two hours S. E. and encamped on another branch of Powder river. We meant to have gone on to the usual encampment the tree alone,[17] but were deterred by a report spread by some of the people who were out yesterday that there was no water in the channel that passes at that place.[18] And to go on farther would be too long. Two large and three small beaver were taken in the traps set last night. Some more were set today. Some tracks of Indians were seen by the hunters, supposed to be Mountain Snakes.[19] In order to secure our horses, We commenced the night guard this evening.

[16] Pierre Depot. He had been with Ogden on the expeditions of 1824–25 and 1825–26.

[17] The lone tree was a famous landmark on the Oregon Trail but was chopped down by an unknown immigrant of 1843. Its exact location is not known. (John Charles Frémont, *Narratives of Exploration and Adventure* [ed. by Allan Nevins], 282.)

[18] The summer of 1830 was unusually dry. Most parties found water at this point—among others, the Frémont expedition. (*Ibid.*)

[19] Mountain Snakes was a name frequently applied to the bands of Northern Paiute living in eastern Oregon. Many early travelers speak of the poverty of these Indians. See July 12, 1831, below.

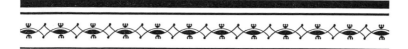

September, 1830

Wedy 1. Blowing fresh. Marched 4¾ hours and encamped near the encampment called the fountain on a small rivulet[1] which scarcely yields a sufficiency of water for our horses to drink. Our course was S. E. 2 hours to past the One Tree on Powder river and 2¾ hours E from there to the encampment. The road good but through a generally barren country, in many places scarcely any thing grows but Wormwood.[2] The after part of the journey not a tree to be seen even on the hills. 1 Large and four small beaver taken.

Thursdy 2. Sultry warm weather till past noon when it blew fresh & became more pleasant.

Continued our route 5½ hours March E. to Burnt river, road gravelly and in places bad, first over a ridge of hills and then down a deep ravine, the country very hilly and broken.[3] Pretty good feeding and plenty of water for the horses. This is a small stream not over 7 to 10 paces wide & not deep. Several of the people were out hunting Kanotta[4] killed two Antelopes. 3 large

---

[1] Possibly Sutton Creek, east of Baker, Oregon. I have been unable to find the spring.

[2] Artemisia.

[3] Later travelers complained at length about this section of the trail.

[4] Louis Kanota (also Kanotta, Kanotte, and Canote), who deserted from

& 2 small beaver were taken by J. Despard[5] and Pichette. Several were off to set traps. I don't like to check their ardour, yet it would be as well were they to pass on without hunting so much after the few straggling beaver that are to be had here, as it fatigues and impoverishes their horses to little purpose and reduces them so much that they will be unable for very active duty when we come to where beaver are more numerous.

Friday 3. Warm weather. Marched about 12 Miles E. by S. along the North side of Burnt river, which we crossed and immediately recrossed to avoid a steep hill, during the day the road bad and lay through a very hilly broke[n] country & generally very barren. Camped at Campment [blank in MS] plenty of water for the horses, but not very good feeding. Short as the days march was several of the horses nearly exhausted and the men much fatigued. The hunters were out but killed no Animals. The traps set last night produced 6 Beaver. In the evening two Snake Indians visited our camp. these are the first Indians we have seen since we left the fort;[6] they have one horse with them. A number of them are encamped a short way ahead.

Satdy 4. Cloudy, blowing fresh. Course the same as yesterday about 14 Miles along the North side of Burnt river to the crossing place[7] where we are to leave it and fall upon the Snake river. The road and appearance of the country the same as yesterday. At our camp we have plenty of water and grass for the

---

Ogden in 1825. (E. E. Rich, ed., *Peter Skene Ogden's Snake Country Journals, 1824–25 and 1825–26,* Vol. XIII [1950] of the Hudson's Bay Record Society Series, 53. Hereafter cited as *HBRS*, XIII.)

[5] Joseph Despard, also Despart. He was with Ogden in 1824–25 *(HBRS,* XIII, 103–104). He later settled in the Willamette Valley.

[6] Work ignores his Cayuse traveling companions and, of course, does not consider Indian hunters and wives traveling as a part of the brigade.

[7] The ford is just upstream from Huntington, Oregon.

horses. Of which they are in much need, as many of the leaner ones are tired out when they get to the camp. Two small beaver were taken. Two large beaver were traded from a Snake Indian.[8]

Sundy 4 [*sic*]. Very warm part of the day. Pursued our rout to Snake river about 4 Miles E. S. E., and along its S bank about 10 miles the same course to the long point where we encamped.[9] The country still hilly and broken, but the hills less elevated & less abrupt than on Burnt river.

This part is reckoned a good place for Chivereau, Several hunters were out, but only one Antelope was killed. The river here is about 200 yards wide and has several islands during the portion of it we have passed.

Mondy 6. Weather as yesterday. Marched about 10 miles, the same course as yesterday to the upper end of the White or Yellow banks, the road indifferent, Country still hilly & broken. Two small beaver were taken. a few Snake Indians that are encamped a short way ahead visited us. From these we learn that the great Snake camp is off to the Buffaloe. This is of advantage to us, as they will be before us and amuse the Blackfeet.[10] We encamped early today to cross A. Carson[11] and party who are to separate from us here and hunt in this neighborhood to the Northward.[12]

---

[8] Trade goods were carried by the brigades for this purpose in addition to the normal supplies of goods for presents for chiefs and rewards for service.

[9] This would put the camp opposite Weiser, Idaho.

[10] Blackfoot war parties raided the middle Snake River Valley, frequently staying through the winter. The brigade was to have several encounters with them. For a good description of such a war party, see James Willard Schultz, *With the Indians in the Rockies.*

[11] Alexander Carson, a colorful figure who came overland with Wilson Price Hunt in 1810. For details, see Alice B. Maloney, "Alexander Carson, Wilhamot Freeman," *OHQ* XXXIX (1938), 16–21.

[12] Following Ogden's advice. See appendix B, below.

Tuesday 7. Weather very warm. Proceeded to the traverse[13] a distance of about 11 Miles, here we encamped in order to cross the river tomorrow. We had thought of proceeding up the south side of the river to Sickly river[14] and hunting the upper part where some beaver are supposed to be, but on further consideration it is deemed more advisable to cross and go up the N. side and hunt some other spots and defer the Big river[15] till the spring, by which some time may be saved. Alex Carson and five men P. Depot, J. Cloutin,[16] J. Sanders,[17] & J. Turner[18] & *Jos J. Bt*[19] Crossed the river this morning and proceeded to the Norward where they are to hunt on the upper parts of Waser[20] and Payette's Rivers[21] and cross the Mountains on some of the branches of Salmon river.[22] They are directed

[13] Approximately seven miles downstream from Payette, Idaho.

[14] Malad River, so named because of the painful seizures resulting from eating beaver trapped in this stream. See October, 1830, note 6.

[15] Snake River. Ogden frequently referred to it as South Branch and it was occasionally called Lewis River.

[16] Jerome Cloutier. A freeman, he had been with Ogden in the Snake Country in 1826–27.

[17] John Alexander Sanders, also listed as Jean Sanders. He later retired and settled in the Willamette Valley.

[18] John Turner was one of the four survivors of the massacre of the Jedediah Strong Smith party on the Umpqua River in 1828. He and Alexander Carson are the two Americans referred to by Work, see August 22–September 1, 1830, note 5.

[19] Joseph J. Baptiste. This man's career is difficult to trace because of the penchant of his superiors for random ordering of his three names. He was with several Snake Country brigades.

[20] Weiser River. It is said to have been named for an otherwise unknown German trapper whose name is usually given as Weyer. Ogden spells the name Waser or Wazer. Bancroft has a fine tale in which he states that the river was named for a miner. (H. H. Bancroft, *The History of Washington, Idaho, and Montana, 1845–1889*, Vol. XXXI [1890] of *The Works of Hubert Howe Bancroft*, 247.) The origin of the name is unknown.

[21] Named for François Payette, a member of this expedition, by Donald McKenzie's Snake Country brigade of 1818 (B 202/a/1, July 28, 1824).

[22] Salmon River, popularly known as the River of No Return. The upper river was a favorite trapping ground of the Snake Country brigades. Two

to be at Ft Nezperces from 5th to 10th of July. This party reduces our numbers 6 Men, 4 Women, and 30 horses. We are
still sufficiently strong it is expected to oppose the Blackfeet
should they be hostily inclined as there is good reason to expect.
It is expected this small [party] will make a good hunt. A
party was sent in this direction [last year] also but being too
late it did not do so well as was anticipated.

Wedy. 8. Weather warm. This day to noon was occupied
crossing the river, there were five channels to cross and two of
them were so deep that only the highest horses could cross the
property without being wet. Some few things of the people's
were wet. Some Indians are encamped here, fishing. They lent
their assistance crossing the river, and furnished us with some
salmon both dry and fresh.

Thursday 9. Warm sultry weather. Marched about 18 Miles
S. S. E. viz 12 Miles along the north bank of the river to the
entrance of Payette's river, and 6 Miles up this river.[23] The
road good, some rich low land along the bank of the Big river,
country hilly to the northward, to the Southward appears little
interrupted with hills. Several Snake Indians visited us both
from below and above our camp. to trade Salmon, cords,[24] &c.
they also changed some horses with the people. Traded 5 large
and 9 small beaver from them. Payette found a horse with one
of them which had been stolen from him three years ago, he

members of this party drowned in the Salmon River while with Work in the
expedition of 1831–32.

[23] This day's travel would put the party opposite New Plymouth, Idaho.

[24] Ogden, traveling in the same vicinity in July of 1827, reported "they
had peel'd the Bark of the Worm Wood it is with this they manufacture their
scoop Nets their lines and ropes for their Horses and it answers well almost
equal to those manufactured with Hemp." K. G. Davies and A. M. Johnson,
eds., *Peter Skene Ogden's Snake Country Journals, 1826–27*, Vol. XXIII
[1961] of the Hudson's Bay Record Society Series, 131. Hereafter cited as
HBRS, XXIII.

immediately took it from the Indian who pleaded hard to get it back or another in its place, he said he did not steal it but got it from another Indian, he got only a knife.

Friday 10. A little breeze of wind which rendered the heat more supportable than these days past. Travelled about 16 miles S by E. along the S bank of Payette's river.[25] A level country & the road good, hills not very high on both sides at some distance. A good many of the horses in the brigade considerably tired when we reached the encampment.

Satdy 11. Warm weather for the season. Marched about 20 Miles S. by E. from Payette's river to read's river,[26] over a height of land which divides the vally the former runs through from the vally through which the latter winds, the country generally barren, but the road good. Mountains appear of considerable height to the Northward, to the Southward it appears a flat country occasionally interrupted with hills. Where we are now encamped is represented to be about 3 days march or 50 miles from the Great Snake river which we left a few days ago;[27] This river is also termed the grand wood river[28] from its having a little poplar wood along its banks during almost its whole length. it is here about 40 yards wide, and pretty

[25] The camp would be opposite Emmett, Idaho.

[26] Boise River. It was frequently called Reed's River by the HBC trappers, for John Reed of the Wilson Price Hunt party whose party of trappers was killed at the mouth of the river. (Alexander Ross, *Adventures of the First Settlers on the Oregon or Columbia River* [ed. by Milo M. Quaife], 298–304. Hereafter cited as Ross, *Adventures.*)

[27] The party would now be near the present community of Middleton, Idaho.

[28] The Boise River was also known as the Riviere du Bois, Riviere Boisee, and Wooded River after Lewis and Clark (Philip Ashton Rollins, ed., *The Discovery of the Oregon Trail. Robert Stuart's Narrative of His Overland Trip Eastward from Astoria in 1812–13* [New York, 1935.] 99n.). A local legend still current erroneously attributes the name Boise to Captain Bonneville. The stream was also known as Reed's River, see note 26 above.

deep. Some patches of timber appear on the Mountains to the Northward, except on the banks of the river not a stick to be seen elsewhere. The river here seems to run from E. by S. to W. by N.

Sundy 12. Hazy sultry weather. Continued our journey along the S. bank of Reads river about 18 miles Easterly.[29] Good feeding for the horses at our camp. Several of the men had traps set, only 1 Otter & 2 beaver were taken. Some of the hunters were also in quest of Chivereau & Antelopes, but without success. A party of Snake Indians visited us in the afternoon from whom we traded 4 large and 5 Small beaver. And some cords.

Monday 13. Fine weather. Proceeded along the North bank of the river about 8 Miles to where it issues from the cut rocks in the hills,[30] and where the road leaves it to cut across to sickly river, here we encamped it being a good feeding place for the horses, which are jaded, and a long days march to make to-morrow. The road was good, country level as yesterday, but the hills to the Northward approaching near it. Traded 8 more beaver from the Snake Indians this morning. the people also changed some horses with them. Several traps were set yesterday and 8 beaver taken this morning. One of the men Auguste Finlay lost a horse yesterday which is the first we have lost since we started, he was seen in the morning and when the camp was nearly starting, but happened to be left afterwards.[31]

Tuesdy 14. Very warm part of the day. Proceeded a short distance along the river which we left and cut across the hills, to a small fountain where we encamped having marched about

[29] This would place the party near or in the present city limits of Boise.

[30] This cut in the rocks is just upstream from Boise. The Oregon Trail later came down off the plain into the bottom land at this point.

[31] The following appears in the margin of the journal opposite this entry: "*Recovered next day."

15

20 Miles S. E.[32] here we found scarcely a sufficiency of water for the horses but pretty good feeding. The Road lay over a hilly country but was good. A short distance to the Northward rises a range of naked rugged hills: to the Southward lies an extensive tract of level country, with here and there a little hill, to the Mountains to the Southward of the Big river.[33] The country has been recently overrun by fire. Scarcely a spot of grass left for the horses to feed. Several of the young men were out hunting but without success. What few Antelopes and Chivereau used to be found here, have probably been driven off by the recent fire. 3 beaver were taken. Several of the horses and some of the people were completely tired when they reached the Camp, as short as the distance was.

Wedy 15. Warm sultry weather. Marched about 13 Miles first S. E. & then E. N. E., the road lay most of the way along a deep vally or gully, very uneven and hilly and fatiguing on the horses. Little water and very indifferent grass where we encamped in the evening. The forepart of the days journey the country has been lately overrun by fire. Some hunters were out but had no success. A stragling Antelope is to be seen but no appearance of any other animal.

Thursdy 16. Weather warm. On account of one of the Women Pichettes' wife being taken in labor we did not move camp today. Some of the people were out hunting but no chivereau or Antelopes were to be found. Kanota & L. Etang[34] who

[32] Probably Indian Creek and at the point of the Oregon Trail crossing place.

[33] The party is now on the Snake River plains. The rugged hills to the north mark the divide of the watershed of the South Fork of the Boise River. The mountains to the southward are the Ruby Mountains.

[34] Pierre L'Etang. He had engaged for the Columbia Department in 1818. He served with the brigade of Alexander Roderick McLeod and had been transferred to the Snake Country brigade. His death, at the hands of the Blackfoot Indians, is recorded below, September 25, 1830.

went a head yesterday & slept out last night, arrived with 7 beaver.

Friday 17. Fine weather. We did not move camp today either for the same cause that detained us yesterday. The woman in the course of the day was delivered of a boy.[35] Several of the people out hunting, but without success.

Satdy 18. Low[er]ing stormy weather. Continued our journey about 16 Miles S. E. over a rugged hilly country the road stony in places. Several of the men slept out with their traps last night. 9 beaver were taken. Read's river or a branch of it [South Fork of the Boise River] runs along behind the hills at a short distance to the Northward nearly parallel with our road. The men saw good marks of beaver but several Indians are encamped on the river fishing salmon and breaking up the beaver lodges with sticks which renders them so wild that it is difficult to kill them. It is a risk leaving the traps set as the Indians would steal them.

Sundy 19. Cloudy stormy weather. Marched about 10 miles S. E. to the little Camas plain.[36] The road lay through a hilly country but was pretty good. Several of the people were out, but few of them set traps owing to the Indians living along the part of Read's river which they visited and having broke the lodges. One beaver was taken.

Mondy 20. Fine weather. Marched about 20 miles E. to the

[35] Edward Pichette. (M. Leona Nichols, *The Mantle of Elias*, 271–72. Hereafter cited as Nichols, *Mantle*.)

[36] South of Bennett, Idaho. Work does not identify the Indians but this territory was continuously occupied by the Bannocks at this time and later. The area is still known as Camas Prairie and was the point of origin of the Bannock Indian War of 1878.

2nd little river in the Big Camass plain.[37] The road hilly the forepart of the day, afterwards flat through patches of stony country; Ridges of mountains in along both on the right hand and the left, these on the left very rugged, and all naked. The plain here may be about 15 Miles wide, the little brook on which we are encamped is a branch of a branch of the Sickly river which runs through the plain from W. to E. The grass very dry, but the horses had plenty of water. Several of the people out hunting. 4 Antelopes were killed, 3 by Kanota & 1 by Thos Tawatcon.[38] 8 Beav[er] were taken. Some of the people who set their traps did not arrive at camp in the evening.

Tuesdy 21. Frost these two mornings past, fine weather during the day. Traveled about 8 Miles E. N. E. to a small river [Corral Creek] on which we encamped some distance from the main stream. The road excellent through a level plain, good feeding and plenty of water for the horses. The people set out in different directions hunting, Some Antelopes were seen in the plain but none killed. 25 Beaver were taken. The Snake Camp is a short distance ahead of us. Some of the hunters fell in with some of them from whom they learned that they had a battle with a party of Blackfeet in this plain a short time ago and took four prisoners which they keep in captivity to kill when our camp which they are waiting for joins them. The rest of the B. feet party fled to the Mountain. Three men, Laforte,[39] Desland,[40] & Longtain[41] who slept out the last two nights ar-

---

[37] Sheep Creek, a branch of Camas Creek. The camp would be near Hill City, Idaho.

[38] Thomas Tewatcon was an Iroquois. He had been with Alexander R. McLeod in 1828 on the expedition to the Umpqua to recover Jedediah Smith's property after the massacre of the majority of that party.

[39] Michel La Forte. He seems to have been a member of the Snake Country expedition continuously from 1824 through 1832.

[40] Jean Desland. He was with Work again in 1831–32.

[41] André Longtain or Lonctain. Both versions of the name are used with

rived in the evening with 14 beaver which they took in Read's river, they represent a good many beaver being in the part of it they saw, but it is thought not enough for the whole camp to go for. One of the above men traded 2 Large and 1 Small beaver from the Snake Indians.

Wedy. 22. Fine weather, frost in the morning.

Did not move camp today in order to allow the people to set their traps as there are some beaver about this place. all hands were out and set traps in different directions. Four men returned to Read's River where they are to remain two nights. Kanota & A. Plant[42] killed each an Antelope. 12 beaver & an otter were taken. This is the first day we have stopped to hunt since we left the fort. We have killed altogether about 100 beaver since we started. Kanota saw some tracks in the Mountain which he supposed to be of a party of Blackfeet. Order is given for the guard to keep a good look out.

Thursdy 23. Overcast fine weather. Made a short encampment of about 8 Miles E. N. E. to another small rivulet which crosses the plain.[43] All hands out at their traps 30 beaver and an Otter were taken, a number that was not expected within this part that has been so frequently hunted. Several small creeks in which most of these beaver are taken are nearly dry except in spots here and there.

Friday 24. Fine weather. Did not raise camp today on ac-

about equal frequency. He had been with Ogden as early as the brigade of 1826–27. He later retired to the Willamette Valley where he raised a large family and became an influential member of the French Prairie community.

[42] Antoine Plante. He was probably the son of Astorian Antoine Plante. He first enlisted in the fur trade in 1828 in the Northwest. He is best known for the ferry he conducted on the Mullan Road at the Spokane River crossing. He became a great favorite with travelers on the Mullan Road.

[43] Soldier Creek. The camp would be near Fairfield, Idaho.

count of one of the men Rocque[44] who has been some time ill with a kind of abcess on his belly, which was opened, this morning gave the poor man great relief. he was scarcely able to move these few days past. In our present mode of life a sick person is wretched indeed as he cannot possibly be properly attended to notwithstanding the trouble and delay occasioned to the rest of the party. The people visited and arranged their traps. 15 Beaver and an Otter were brought to the camp besides 8 beaver and an otter which the men who have traps in advance left in cache. A Plante & an Indian Pichette's brother in law[45] killed each an Antelope.

Satdy 25. Fine weather. Marched about 14 Miles E. N. E. to a little river [Willow Creek], where we encamped, near the mountains. The people were out in different directions hunting. At 3 P. M. about an hour and a half after we encamped One of the men T. Tewatcon came running to the Camp afoot almost out of his senses with fear and related that as he, P L'Etang, Baptiste[46] and Kanota's slave[47] were going to visit their traps on this little river in the mountains they were set upon by a war party of Blackfeet[48] and his three companions killed on

[44] George Ross *dit* Rocque. Although he is not mentioned in the published version of the 1831–32 journal, he was with Work that year and again in 1832–33.

[45] He may have been one of the youths mentioned as able to bear arms. See above entry for August 22 and note.

[46] Baptiste Tyaquariche, also known as Baptiste the Iroquois. He deserted from Ogden to the Americans on January 30, 1826 (*HBRS*, XIII, 260). He deserted from this party to the Americans on April 16, 1831 (see entry that date below).

[47] This is, undoubtedly, the slave mentioned as armed (see entry for August 22 above). The company disapproved of Indian slavery but many of the men had slaves. The slaves were said to belong to the Indian wife of the man. (Frederick Merk, *Fur Trade and Empire. George Simpson's Journal, 1824–1825,* 352–56. Hereafter cited as Merk, *Fur Trade and Empire.*)

[48] This was probably the remainder of the war party mentioned above (see entry for September 21). This war party was to plague the brigade during its entire stay in the Snake River plain.

the spot and that it was with the utmost difficulty he escaped. At this time very few of the men were in the camp but some of them soon arrived when we put ourselves in the best state of defense we could, and made pens for our horses. Some parties scoured the hills to discern the enemy, but not knowing exactly where the murder was committed did not proceed to the place but three Caiouse Indians who accompany us found it and found poor L'Etang and the slave murdered as stated and stripped of their clothing and the latter scalped. But Baptiste was still alive and they brought him to the camp when dark. He is wounded in the knee but apparently not dangerously. he is much more collected than Thomas and gives the following account of the Melancholy occurence. The whole four were ascending a pretty steep hill afoot leading their horses and not paying proper attention to the sides of the road, when the Indians suddenly started up from the concealment among some grass and small bushes, and instantly fired upon them, then he received his wound. the Indians rushed upon him and seized him, but not before he discharged his gun and killed one of them. he called to the slave who was near him to fire which he did when the Indians left Baptiste and rushed upon him and killed him while they were thus employed Baptiste continued to run some distance and conceal himself in a tuft of willows, where he remained unobserved till the Cayouses found him. Poor L'Etang seemed to make no defence but attempted to escape hence it is probable he was severely wounded the first fire. The slave, Baptiste thinks, killed one when he fired and when they seized him struggled hard for his life which detained the Indians so long that Baptiste had time to escape & hide himself. Thomas was fortunate in not being wounded his pursuers were very near coming up with him and probably would have taken him had they not given up the pursuit on hearing the report of Kanota's rifle fired at a deer at no great distance, and as is supposed seeing our people moving to the encampment at the same time. Probably to these circumstances is also owing Baptist's safety, for immediately on dispatching and rifling the other two unfortunate men they precipitately made off without taking time to cut up and mangle the bodies as they are barbarously wont to do. they scalped only the slave. The Cayouse's state that L Etang received a ball in the neck, one in the head and two or three in the body. Baptiste thinks the party might consist of about 30 men. These relentless, blood thirsty savages could have no other motive for committing this attrocious murder but to possess themselves of the mens horses, arms and clothing. The slave's horse ran off and was found and brought to our camp in the evening. Two others of the horses are supposed also to have ran off to the Mountains or the plains, so that the barbarians have got only one horse, three guns, (for they took Baptist's) and the clothing of the two men they killed besides what traps they may have stolen. Another of the men Champaigne[49] who had his traps not so far up the river, had a narrow escape. The tracks of the Indians were quite fresh they stole three of his traps. Thus are the people wandering through this country in quest of beaver continually in danger of falling into the hands of these ruthless savages and certain of losing their lives in the most barbarous manner, independent of the privations and hardships of every other kind they subject themselves to.[50] The men generally risk too much. As the Snake Camp is ahead of us it was thought the Blackfeet would be hanging on their rear and few remaining in this neighbourhood. the tracks of this party here were seen when the people came first to set their traps in this river. Some tracks have also

[49] François Champaigne. He had first served in the Northwest at Fort George (Astoria, Oregon). He was with Ogden in 1826–27 and he retired to become a Willamette settler in 1841.

[50] Work did not copy this bitter sentence into his copy of the journal which he sent to London. That account of the fight is also shorter and more matter of fact, therefore less interesting.

been seen along the river in the plain but whether of Blackfeet or Snakes is not certain.

27 Beaver and an Otter were taken today

Sundy 26. Fine weather. Did not move camp today. Sent Payette and 12 men to inter our unfortunate companions that came to such an untimely end yesterday. Poor L Etang was shot in the head, neck, belly and wrist and had received an arrow in the thigh. The Slave had also received several wounds, and seems to have struggled hard for his life. A gun was found lieing near him broke at the guard, and loaded with two balls but no powder.[51] fragments of another gun, thought to be that of the Slave were found strewed about the place. The Blackfeet seem to have made a precipitate retreat as several articles were found which they threw away such as parchment shields or Arrowfinders,[52] and some articles of clothing, besides a number of cords and whips, always appendages of horse thieves. From the tracks the men judge the party to be more numerous than was first supposed. They have stolen and carried of[f] 25 traps, viz. 9 from Kanotta, 5 from the late L'Etang, 8 from the 2 Iroquois, and 3 from Champaigne besides 8 or ten beaver which the men put in cache the last time they visited the traps. The men suppose they had been lieing in wait for the people all the day before.

The four men who went to Read's river on the 22nd arrived with 27 beav[er] & 1 Otter, the produce of their hunt since then. Two men also arrived that had slept out below. Brought to the camp altogether 42 beaver & 2 otters.

[51] A common mistake with muzzle-loaders in action. Studies of the American Civil War have shown this to be an amazingly frequent error in combat, even among experienced troops.

[52] This unusual term may be Indian in origin. Work tended to translate literally and the term may have come from his Indian wife, but I have found no informants on the Spokane reservation who could identify such a term.

Monday 27. Fine weather. The wounded man Baptiste requiring a little repose we did not move camp today. Several of the men set traps. 9 Beaver were brought to the camp besides some that were left in cache below. Some more tracks of Indians supposed to be Blackfeet were seen. Some of the people are getting discouraged on account of the danger to which they are exposed, when they used to pass this road it was later in the season and few Blackfeet were to be seen. Sold the property of the late P. L'Etang by auction.[53]

Tuesdy 28. Frost in the night fine weather afterwards. Moved camp and marched 12 or 14 Miles E. S. E. and encamped on the N. branch of Sickly river[54] a little below where it receives the Camass plain river, The country becoming rugged and barren in appearance the low ground studded with patches of bleak stoney ground. The road in places stony & hard on the horses feet. This branch of the river is but a small stream. but has the appearance of a good many beaver.

Several of the men set some more traps, the few that were in the water produced 10 beaver and an Otter. The tracks of parties of Blackfeet were observed who are supposed to have been prowling about our camp in the night, but from the dryness of the ground it is difficult to know exactly whether the tracks are quite fresh or a few nights old. A smoke was observed in the mountain yesterday evening. A strict watch is kept both day and night, and the horses tied up in the night. This is a great inconvenience to us the nights are so long that the horses have not time to feed. moreover the grass is in general bad. It will therefore be out of our power to proceed as expeditiously as we wish as we must allow the horses time to

[53] A standard procedure when out in the mountains. The proceeds of the auction were credited to his account with the company. Should his account show a favorable balance, this amount was paid to his heirs.

[54] Wood River. The camp would be in what is now the upper end of Magic Reservoir.

feed or they will become so lean that they will not be able to go on or become so weak that they will die in the winter. We are put to all this trouble and inconvenience by these villainous Blackfeet.

Wedy 29. Fine weather. Proceeded about 18 miles S. S. E. down the river. The country not hilly but in places rugged and stony, scarcely any thing to be seen but wormwood. The road in places very stony and bad for the horses feet. The river is in places flat with some poplar and willows growing along its banks, and in places it is confined in a narrow channel between steep rocks. Where there is any wood or willows there is beaver. Antelopes are also numerous here, the tracks of Elk are also seen. Some of the hunters also observed the tracks of buffaloe not very old. 24 beavers were taken.

Thursdy 30. Fine weather. Did not move camp today to allow the people to examine the river and let the traps remain. 20 Beaver were taken. Some of the people descended the river a long encampment, and report the country as very stony. the river also stony little or no wood and scarcely the mark of a beaver. I had intended to descend this river to its junction with the great Swamp river [Little Wood River] which we meant to ascend, but the report of the badness of the road and little signs of beaver renders it necessary to alter the plan and proceed to the Grand Muskeg hu[nt] down the river and return the same road. Passing down this river through such a stony coun try would much injure the horses' feet and disable them from work which would be a great loss. One of the hunters saw the tracks of three buffalo quite fresh, and the tracks of 5 more only a few days old. Where we are at present encamped there is but little feeding for the horses, and their having nothing to eat in the night, is reducing them much in flesh.

October, 1830

Friday 1. Fine weather. Returned back about 6 miles the same road we passed two days ago and encamped on a good point for feeding the horses which they are in much need of. The encampment would have been too long to have struck straight across to the great swamp moreover the road would have been more stony than from this place. 3 Beaver were taken. The tracks of four Indians were seen near the camp last night, but it is not certain whether they are Blackfeet or Snakes, however there is little doubt they are horse thieves seeking an opportunity to steal.

Satdy 2. Fine weather. Marched about 14 miles N by E. to the Great Swamp where we encamped about the middle or rather towards the lower end of it. Our road pretty good but in places stony, and in the forepart of the day thick wormwood, the road through the hills pretty level. This Swamp is an extensive valley or plain surrounded by steep hills on almost every side, here the north branch of Sickly river has its source,[1] at different places, at the very commencement the water is clear and a pretty strong current at the very place where it issues. though called a swamp except along the edges of the brook the ground is hard, the surrounding hills are destitute of wood,

[1]Wood River has its source many miles to the north of this swamp, which is at the junction of Camas Creek and Wood River.

and only some tufts of willows poplar and birch are to be seen though the swamp, except at its upper end where a strip of wood resembling a river appears.[2] We are encamped in an excellent situation. The people setting their traps but very little signs of beaver, this place having so frequently hunted and lately too, it can scarcely be expected to be otherwise. Three beaver were taken at our camp this morning.

Sundy 3. Frost in the morning fine weather afterwards. Continued our course down the river about 16 miles nearly E. The road part of the way stony afterwards through a level plain. The river though narrow, is in places deep winding through the plain like a canall and from the steepness of the banks difficult to cross. In places tufts of willows and in other places only grass along its margin, in some places runs over a stony bottom. The men complain that no great signs of beaver are to be seen, but they say we are not yet arrived at the places where the beaver are. 8 beaver & 1 Otter were taken today. The tracks of four Indians were seen near our camp this morning, probably the same Indians here a few nights ago still sculking about to steal.

Mondy 4. Frost in the morning, warm afterwards. Marched about 16 miles South, down the river, the road pretty good through a barren sandy country thickly studded with stony patches. The river pretty rapid running over a stony bottom, only here and there some tufts of willows. We are still said not to have reached the beaver part of the river. The men were all out setting their traps. 10 Beaver were taken. Kanotta & C. Plant[3] killed each an Antelope yesterday, these animals are numerous yet the hunters were unsuccessful.

[2] Probably the bed of the river, dry in the late fall. Previous entries make it apparent that this was an unusually dry year.

[3] Charles Plante. Plante was from St. Cuthbert, District of Montreal.

Tuesdy 5. Fine weather. Our course was this day West about 16 miles. The road pretty level but in places very stony, indeed the country particularly on the South side of the river very stony but level. 17 beaver were taken. We are now said to have reached the valley where beaver were expected to have been found numerous, yet there appears little prospects of our expectations being realized. A small party of hunters 11 years ago took 300 beaver in two short encampments about this place and then not cleanly hunted, and it is not known to have been hunted since. The hunters concur in opinion that beaver are very scarce at present, from what cause there is a great difference of opinion. Some think the scarcity is occasioned by a fire which overran the country here some years back, marks of which still remain. Others think that they have been destroyed by some distemper, besides which different other causes are assigned. Some destroying distemper is the most probable cause of their disappearance. There is no doubt they were formerly very numerous the banks of the river are in many places hollow by their old holes. There being little willows and only reeds many places along the bank their lodges are not numerous, but their holes in abundance everywhere. 17 Beaver were taken.

Wedy 6. Weather fine. Did not move camp today in order to allow the hunters to set their traps and examine the river. Some of the men went to a considerable distance down the river to where rocky dalls commence.[4] no beaver marks worth mentioning to be seen, though this portion of the river is where we expected to find them most abundant. As nothing worth while is to be obtained it is unnecessary to proceed farther down the river we shall therefore return back upon our road tomor-

---

A veteran of the Snake Country brigade, he was to end his trapping career as a member of Michel Laframboise's California party. He retired to become a Willamette settler.

[4] Near the mouth of Little Wood River.

row. 12 beaver were taken. Several of the people were sick from eating of the beaver. The river about here and indeed farther up is burdened with reeds, on the roots of which the beaver feed, but whether it is these or other roots that communicate the quality of sickening the people to their flesh it is not easy to say. hemlock[5] is also found Along the river the roots of which they are said to eat indeed they may feed upon different other roots and plants which may escape the notice of the hunters. The leaves of the reeds particularly and some other plants are covered with a glutinous *saccarine* substance sweet to the taste, which adheres to everything that touches it, the clothes of the hunters who pass through the reeds are covered with it. The leaves are also covered generally on the under side with innumerable swarms of green insects somewhat in shape & size resembling lice.[6] They are so thick that they are floating in clouds down the river.

Thursdy 7. Still fine weather. Returned about 6 miles up the river the same road we came two days ago. 7 Beaver & an Otter were taken.

---

[5] This would be *Cicuta douglasi. Cicuta maculata*, or water hemlock, is related to *Cicuta douglasi* and similar in appearance but is not native to this region. This plant may be the cause of the scarcity of beaver. After the fire mentioned above, vegetation would be scarce. *Cicuta douglasi*, an early plant, would probably be the first vegetation available. The survivors would have an immunity and, probably, a certain amount of the poison in their systems. Eating the beaver, then, could produce the illness described, which sounds like a mild case of hemlock poisoning in its symptoms.

Suggestions by one author that water of the stream flowing over the roots of the plants would carry the poison are ridiculous for reasons that should require no explanation.

Detailed studies of the beaver have not been made. A captive beaver fed with roots in small quantities showed no ill effects. Unfortunately (for science), execution and autopsy were not possible to determine if the poison remained in the animal's system.

[6] Plant lice, an aphidida very common in the Rocky Mountain region.

29

Friday 8. Weather overcast. Did not move camp today in order to allow our horses to feed of which many of them are in much want, being kept up every night they are 12 hours out of 24 without eating which together with the dryness and scarcity of the grass are rendering many of them very lean. As few Indians are about this neighborhood we can let them feed with more safety. Moreover it is wished to delay a little so that the Blackfeet may have gone on after the Snake camp, and quitted the mountains before we cross them to the Salmon river where we intend to go. The Blackfeet will suppose we have gone on to Snake River and will not expect us back this road. No tracks of Indians are seen here except that of solitary Snake family on the day we descended to our last camp, and they made off immediately on our approach.

Satdy 9. During the first watch last night there was a storm of thunder and a very heavy shower of rain. The weather cool during the day. Continued our rout about 8 miles up the river and encamped in a pretty good feeding place for the horses. Some of the men had their traps set and took 4 beaver. during the storm in the first watch last night an Indian got unperceived among the horses which he frightened twice and sent them off and though they were hobbled it was with difficulty they were got stopped. he however did not succeed in his attempt to steal though he bridled one of them with a willow.[7] Notwithstanding a strict search he could not be found.

Sunday 10. Cloudy weather a good deal of thunder and some light rain. Continued our rout up the river about 10 or 12 miles. Several of the people were out with their traps 5 beaver were taken. One of the hunters who was farthest up the river brought

[7] The Indian method of bridling was to loop a cord or thong around the lower jaw. A willow switch freshly cut would serve as well for a short period of time.

the news that he had met a party of 20 American hunters who had arrived from the Snake river and were two days without water.[8] One of them Frizzon an Iroquoy who formerly deserted from us came to our camp[9] but little news was obtained from him as it was late when he arrived, and what he did tell appears to have little truth in it. One of the women forgot something this morning and after being off some distance from the camp returned for it. An Indian was crouching among the grass and was observed starting up with a bent bow. the woman made off and escaped, he was on the opposite side of the little river or probably she would not have got off but been murdered for her horse & clothes.

Monday 11. Fine weather. Continued our course and encamped a little above our encampment of the 3rd Inst. No beaver were taken today though several traps were in the water. The Americans encamped within a short distance of us. Some of their men came to our camp and some of ours visited theirs.[10]

Tuesdy 12. Frost in the night, fine weather afterwards.
Left Sickly river and struck across the plain along the foot of the Mountains N. N. E. about 16 Miles to a small river which bears the name of Bercier[11] to the Westward lies a ridge

---

[8] An American Fur Company party led by Joseph Robidoux. It had separated into two groups at American Falls. This party was sent to the Malad (Wood) River to hunt. (Warren A. Ferris, *Life in the Rocky Mountains* [ed. by J. Cecil Alter], 53–56. Hereafter cited as Ferris, *Life in the Rocky Mountains.*)

[9] I have been unable to identify this man. It is probable that he was one of the three deserters from the Fraeb-Gervais party of the Rocky Mountain Fur Company who had been signed by Robidoux shortly before this (*ibid.*, 53).

[10] Ferris relates that a friend learned of L'Etang's death at this time (*ibid.*, 53).

[11] Probably Silver Creek. This stream was probably named for Pierre Bercier, who was a member of this expedition. He had been with Ogden in the Snake Country as early as 1826–27.

of rugged hills and to the Eastward the extensive plain toward the Snake river. Some Indians were sculking about our camp last night seeking an opportunity to steal. One of the men going for some water when dark saw or thought he saw an Indian in the river with his head above water. the alarm was given but he could not be found though a strict search was made. Our object now is to reach Salmon river with as little delay as possible. There are two roads, nearly the same in length, that by the North branch of Sickly river[12] and the one we are taking by Goddins river.[13] we are induced to prefer the latter as being more level and easier for the horses, and as we may a little sooner find buffaloe so that we may get some provisions which is much wanted, as several of the people are entirely out of food. Moreover by this rout the party of Americans may not be inclined to follow us not knowing what road we are taking,[14] or perhaps may not be able to follow us as their horses appear to be very lean, and they have not two per man, they have however no families or lodges and apparently very little baggage to embarrass them which gives them infinitely the advantage over us, as to expedition of movement. nevertheless we still expect to keep ahead of them. By this road also we may probably fall in with the Bannack Snake Camp[15] and obtain a few furs in trade.

The Americans raised camp before us in the morning and proceeded up the river but on seeing us strike across the country

[12] This route goes up Wood River nearly to Ketchum. It then follows Trail Creek past Sun Valley and thence down the Big Lost River.

[13] Big Lost River, so called because it disappears into the Snake River plains. It was named for Henry Goddin, who was killed there in 1830. (Alexander Ross, *The Fur Hunters of the Far West*, II, 124-25.)

[14] Unknown to Work, the American party planned to return to Cache Valley in Utah for the winter, a frequent wintering spot for American trappers (Ferris, *Life in the Rocky Mountains*, 53).

[15] The Bannocks were a branch of the Northern Paiute. They ranged eastern Idaho and southwestern Montana and west to eastern Oregon. (Brigham D. Madsen, *The Bannock of Idaho*, 17.)

they also left the river and followed us along the foot of the mountains and encamped some distance behind us in a little river where Payette and party were defeated two years ago.[16] I did not see a Mr. Robbidou[17] who is at the head of this party, but from the intercourse our people had with their men it appears this party consists of 20 men, that the whole party of their hunters amount to upwards of 100 men, (perhaps they exaggerate,)[18] that Crooks and company[19] are the principal outfitters and Mr. Fontanelle[20] who manages their affairs is now at Snake River with a party of 50 men.[21] That they have a large quantity of goods in Cache, But that there are several petty Bourgeois in the party with a few men on their own accounts. They have been hunting part of the summer on the upper part of the Snake River. A party of their hunters were defeated last fall by the Blackfeet on the Yellowstone river and 18 men killed. They intended to have gone on to the F

[16] This probably refers to the encounter briefly mentioned by Ogden in his journal of the 1827–28 expedition as occurring in May, 1828 (T. C. Elliott, ed., "Journal of Peter Skene Ogden; Snake Expedition, 1827–28," *OHQ*, XI [1910], 378).

[17] Joseph Robidoux. He was a principal trader with the American Fur Company until his retirement from the trade in 1831. Following retirement he founded the city of St. Joseph, Missouri.

[18] There were only fifty-seven men in the party when Work met it in April, 1831. See entry for April 14, 1831, below.

[19] Crooks and Company is an anachronism, as Ramsay Crooks was manager of the Western Department of the American Fur Company until 1834, when he purchased the Northern Department of the company from John Jacob Astor (Hiram Martin Chittenden, *The American Fur Trade of the Far West*, I, 365, 380). It would, however, be natural for the trappers to refer to the company under the name of the St. Louis manager, who would represent the ultimate authority to them.

[20] Lucien Fontanelle was a famous brigade leader for the American Fur Company (*ibid.*, 389). He had a long and illustrious career.

[21] Fontanelle seems to have been in Utah at this time. This report to Work was probably some more of the exaggeration he suspected (Ferris, *Life in the Rocky Mountains*, 47, 51).

Heads[22] this fall but were deterred from doing so by considering the season too far advanced.

Wedy. 13. Blowing fresh. Proceeded up the river about 10 miles through a deep valley between steep hills. This is a small stream [Fish Creek], with some poplar and willows upon it and appears well adapted for beaver, yet very few are in it. Some traps were set in the lower part of it yesterday evening & six beaver taken. The road in places passed over some steep parts of hills but was in general good. The people were out hunting, but killed nothing. Several recent tracks of buffaloe were seen both yesterday and today, but none of the animals seen. The Snake camp passed this road not long since. We expect that by taking this road in preference to going around the mountains by the plain we will save one or two days march. We saw nothing of the Americans nor were any Indians observed about our camp last night.

Thursdy 14. Blowing pretty fresh. Fine weather. Continued our journey about 16 miles, viz 10 miles N by E up a narrow steep ravine to the height of land, and 6 miles down another deep gully along a small branch of Goddin's river to its junction with a larger branch [Antelope Creek]. From the steepness and ruggedness of the road this was a fatiguing day on the horses and harrassing on the people. The people were out in the Mountains hunting and killed 4 bulls, viz. C. Plant 1, P Finlay[23] 1 & Payette & A. Finlay 1. A considerable portion of the meat was brought to the camp and a seasonable supply to many of the people it was. 5 Beaver were taken in the morning.

[22] Flathead Indians, a Salishan tribe of western Montana. The tribe was a favorite with the trappers and had been visited by American parties for several years.

[23] Pinesta Finlay. He was another son of Jacques Rafael "Jacco" Finlay. In 1838 he was a freeman living in the Willamette Valley.

34

Friday 15. Some Showe[r]s in the night. Fine weather during the day.

Marched about 20 miles N. E. along this branch to its junction with Goddin's river,[24] where we encamped the horses being much fatigued. The road pretty good the forepart of the day through plains and swamps and afterwards through a barren country covered with wormwood, with scarcely any grass to be seen. This part of the river winds through a small valley with naked hills on both sides, at this fork the valley is of considerable extent. Where we are encamped is a small swampy plain, where there has been a good deal of grass, but which is almost entirely eat up by buffalo and the horses of the Snake Indians who have been not long since [undecipherable] encamped here. A Buffalo cow & a bull were killed, four buffalo were seen. 2 beaver were taken.

Satdy 16. Fine weather. Marched about 7 Miles W. N. W. up the river where we encamped for the double purpose of allowing the horses to feed and to kill some buffalo, which were feeding in the plain.[25] Some cows were killed. 8 Beaver were taken this morning.

Sundy 17. Fine weather, frost in the morning. Continued our journey 15 miles W. N. W. up the river, the road good and pretty level, steep hills on both sides of the vally, along the river it is occasionally swampy with some poplar and willows, farther up the country is covered with wormwood.

The hunters were out and killed several buffaloe of which a large herd was found near the camp and some more ahead. 2 beaver were taken.

---

[24] The party would be near Darlington on the Union Pacific line to Mackay, Idaho.

[25] The party would be camped near Mackay, Idaho.

Mondy 18. Raw cold weather. Marched about 11 Miles and encamped in a swamp where there is pretty good feeding for the horses. The appearance of the country the same as yesterday, scarcely a blade of grass is left in most places by the buffaloe. The hunters killed several cows. 2 beaver were taken this morning.

Tuesdy 19. Fine weather. Did not move camp today, in order to allow the people time to dry their provisions. The hunters killed some more buffaloe.

Wedy 20. Raw cold weather, blowing fresh from the Northward.

Marched 10 miles W. N. W. to what is called the fountain which is nothing more than a swamp, where Goddin's river has its source.[26] The road good. Country the same appearance as these days past. At this place the plain extends to a considerable width, here there is a road to the Northward through a cut in the mountains leading to Day's defile.[27] Also a road falls in from the Southward from the head of Sickly river, this is the road which we left on the 12th Inst. At our encampment there is not a bit of wood, so that Wormwood is used for fuel. The men had a fine hunt in the afternoon after a herd of buffalo several of whom they killed. Some time back these animals have been exceedingly numerous here, but the Bannack Snakes having passed but very short [time] ago have driven most of them off.

Thursdy 21. Raw cold weather. Marched 12 Miles W. by N. over a height of land to another swamp or Fountain where

---

[26] Thousand Springs. This is not, however, the source of this river.

[27] Day's Defile is the canyon of the Little Lost River. The stream and canyon were named for Astorian John Day, who died here with a Snake Country brigade in winter camp on February 16, 1820.

a branch of Salmon river has its rise [Warm Spring Creek]. The road lay over one or two little hills along a valley and was good. In places the hills on both sides of the road very rugged & steep, here and there a little wood is seen thinly scattered over them. Some of the high peaks have patches of Snow since the past winter. The men drove down a small herd of buffalo from the Mountains and killed several of them but they were so lean that they were not worth the trouble. Immense herds have been seen in this valley very recently but at present few are to be seen.

Friday 22. Weather Milder than these days past, rained a little in the night, some of the higher hills grey with Snow. Marched 18 Miles N. W. to Salmon river, the road in places hilly but good lay along a valley which at the river spreads out to a plain of considerable extent. Surrounded with rugged hills. The river here is divided into different channels and is pretty large, it here runs from the S. W. here are also two small branches that fall in from the Westward. Here is also a hot spring.[28] The river has a good deal of poplar and willows on its banks, but the plains are exceedingly barren and scarcely a blade of grass left by the buffalo. Some of the men set their traps, there is the appearance of beaver. Some buffalo were killed. Salmon ascend this branch to past this place. The Banack Snakes have been lately encamped here, but have taken another direction and cut across the hills to the N. E.

Satdy 23. Blowing fresh but not cold. Did not move camp today in order to allow the people to set their traps, which the most of them did. 8 beaver were taken in the few traps set yesterday.

[28] One of the streams would be Garden Creek in Challis, Idaho. The hot spring is on the east bank of the river and was a well-known and frequently mentioned landmark of the pioneer period.

37

Sundy 24. Cloudy Raw cold weather. Moved camp to across the river a distance of 3 or 4 miles to a better feeding place for the horses.[29] 30 beaver were taken.

Mondy 25. Heavy rain forepart of the day. The higher Mountains white with snow. On account of the unfavourable weather did not raise camp today. 19 beaver were taken, which the men reckon few considering the number of traps set and the good places [at which they were set.

Tuesdy 26. Weather fair but cold. Struck into the Mountains and proceeded about 16 Miles in a S. W. direction to a small creek *in a deep valley* where we encamped for the night. The road though not bad lay over a hilly uneven country, and in order to reach water we had to make a long days march. Many of the horses were nearly knocked up, and the people also fatigued. The country is becoming woody which renders passing through a hilly country still more difficult. The valley where we are now encamped affords but indifferent feeding for the horses and not much of it. Our object in taking this road is to hunt on some forks which were visited by some of Mr. Ross'[30] freem[en] about 7 years ago and where a good many beaver are supposed to be. The distance is stated to be about 6 days march. From the information of those acquainted with the country it is expected we may pass 20 to 30 days in that quarter and still be out in sufficient time to hunt down the branch we left this morning, and have time to reach a situation to winter in before too much snow falls. The men took up their traps this morning and found only 7 beaver in them.

29 The camp appears to have been at the present site of Challis, Idaho.

30 Alexander Ross. He led the Snake Country expedition of 1823–24. He had started with the 1824 expedition but was replaced by Ogden. He was then appointed to the Missionary Society School at Red River (Merk, *Fur Trade and Empire*, 351).

Wedy 27. Raw cold weather sharp frost in the night the little river where we were encamped frozen over and ice sufficiently strong to bear ones weight. Continued our journey about 8 or 10 miles W. the road lay up a deep ravine and over a steep mountain. it was in many places very stony and nearly barred up with fallen timber. Short as the days journey is the horses are completely jaded and the people much exhausted. We missed the proper pass of the mountain which rendered crossing it more difficult than it otherwise would have been. it was so exceedingly steep, that the horses could scarcely keep their feet. Where we are encamped on a small rivulet there is scarcely a mouthful of food for the horses. From the top of the mountain there is nothing to be seen but mountains and deep narrow ravines as far as the eye can reach and the country wooded, except here and there on the tops of the mountains. The road we mean to pursue lies along this little rivulet through a deep valley. the road is represented as not bad and the country affords some pasture for the horses, there are two other mountains to pass. after passing the first there is a plain country and plenty of excellent feeding for the horses. Notwithstanding this from the advanced state of the season in these high regions it is considered that the small rivulets will be frozen so that the beaver cant be taken. Moreover there is a danger of a fall of snow preventing us from returning, from these considerations it is deemed most prudent to return, and make what we can on the lower rivers before the winter sets in.

Thursdy 28. Keen frost in the night, about an inch deep of snow fell with a squall of wind. Returned the same road we went yesterday and camped near the same place.

Friday 29. Raw cold weather, half a foot deep of snow fell in the night. Marched about 8 miles on our return the same road we passed two days ago.

Satdy 30. Cold but fine clear weather, frost in the night. Continued our journey and encamped in the valley near our station of the 26th. here there is no snow and apparently a different climate.

Sunday 31. Slight frost in the night, fine weather. Marched about 10 Miles North down the river,[31] the road pretty good. Country barren except small spots along the river side, the river runs down a deep valley steep hills on both sides. The river here is 15 to 20 yards wide. Buffalo have been here in considerable numbers not long since, but none are to be seen near. The rocks abound with grey sheep.[32] Our hunters saw several herds but killed only 3.

[31] Near the mouth of Morgan Creek.
[32] Bighorn sheep, *Ovis canadensis.*

November, 1830

Mondy 1. Blew a storm with some heavy rain in the night. Raw cold weather during the day.

This being All Saints day and a fast & holiday with the Canadians we did not raise camp.

Tuesdy 2. Cloudy cold weather. Proceeded down the river about 8 miles North to a fork which falls in from the Eastward [Pahsimeroi River]. This branch lies down a fine valley and heads of it are separated from Day's river [Little Lost River] by a little height of land. Our road today was very rugged and stony and lay over a number of deep gullies. At this fork the country is flat for a short distance on both sides of the river. Here we met two F. Head Indians who say they were out looking for white people. The F. Head camp is about 6 days journey off. it is very strong, the F. Heads, Pd Oreilles,[1] Nezperces,[2] & Spokans,[3] being all together.

Wedy 3. Weather milder than these days past. Continued

[1] Pend d'Oreilles, a Salishan tribe inhabiting northern Idaho.

[2] Nez Percé, a Shahaptian people whose territory extended from the upper Salmon River in Idaho west into the Blue Mountains and north to include the Clearwater River in Idaho.

[3] Spokanes, a Salishan tribe of eastern Washington. Work's wife, Josette Legacé, was a Spokane. Such a coalition of tribes as mentioned here was a common defensive measure during this period when hunting in an area subject to Blackfeet raiding parties (Haines, *Red Eagles*, 26).

our journey down the river about 8 miles North, the road here is much frequented large parties of Indians passing, but it is exceedingly bad very stony lying over steep rocks and hills and very harrassing both on the horses and people. the horses becoming very lean and their hoofs worn out. The men were out in different directions in search of beaver. there are some small rivulets fall into the river but it is difficult to ascend them on account of the ruggedness of the country. Some *signs* of beaver are to be seen. 15 were taken these three days past. In the lower part of the fork we left this morning, there is snow. 3 or 4 sheep were killed.

Thursdy 4. Cloudy cold weather. Continued our rout about 8 miles farther down the river the same course as yesterday.[4] 5 beaver & 1 Otter were taken. C Plant found a valley a considerable way up a small river which falls in from the Westward, where there are a good many beaver. he returned to it with 4 other men. Several of the other men have gone down the river to set their traps. The river is beginning to assume a better appearance for beaver.

Friday 5. Blew a hurricane in the night with snow & very cold. Weather milder during the day but continues cold. Did not raise camp today waiting for Plant and party they arrived in the evening with 29 beaver which with the 12 taken by those at camp make 41. The traps are left in the water, the little creek is very small and beginning to freeze up.

Satdy 6. Cloudy cold weather. Continued our route about 10 miles down the river which is still north, little change in the road. Two of the men M. Finlay[5] and A Plant arrived after

---

[4] This camp site is approximately eight miles north of Ellis, Idaho.

[5] Miquam Finlay, who also seems to have been a son of "Jacco" Finlay and brother to the other two Finlays with this party. He was with Work again the following year.

an absence of 5 days in the mountains hunting. they brought only 7 beaver. they saw the appearance of a good many but the small streams are freezing up. There were in all 16 beaver taken. The two F Head Indians returned to their camp. I sent a little tobacco *by* them *to* the chiefs. I also sent a letter to Mr. C. F. M Loughlin[6] apprising him of our progress.

Sunday 7. Mild weather. Did not raise camp today waiting for the men that were behind. they arrived in the evening with 9 beaver, they say more are in the river but it is getting frozen over so that they cant take them. A Finlay killed 3 sheep.

Mondy 8. Stormy with some rain in the night. Cloudy cold weather during the day. Marched about 8 miles down the river to the traverse, here in consequence of an impassable rock the river has to be crossed and the road lies on the W. side. The road less hilly today but if anything more stony than usual. Several of the men had traps set. Only 6 beaver & 2 Otters were taken.

Tuesdy 9. Fine weather. Marched about 7 Miles N by W. down the river and encamped at a good feeding place for the horses.[7] A little distance above the fork of the river [Lcmhi River] The road good having but few stones. The banks of the river flat and in places swampy and well wooded, principally with poplar and willows. The mountains a little farther from the river than these days past. Two small streams fall in from the Westward. In this valley which extends from here to some distance below the forks where the river is again enclosed with rocks and mountains we expected to have found a good many

---

[6] Dr. John McLoughlin, of course. The initials above stand for his rank, chief factor. Work's letter arrived at Fort Vancouver on March 8, 1831 (Barker, *McLoughlin Letters*, 185).

[7] Opposite Salmon, Idaho.

beaver, but have the mortification of being disappointed, as very few are to be found. there are marks of their having been numerous in the early part of the season, but a large camp of Nezperces passed a portion of the summer here, some of whom employed themselves hunting beaver and have either killed the greater part of them or rendered them so shy that they are difficult to be taken. The traps produced 8 beaver and 2 Otters. Several of the men out hunting and killed some sheep, Ant. Hoole[8] killed a sheep in the mountain on the other side of the river opposite the camp at no great distance, and was employed skinning it when he discovered several Blackfeet close to and nearly surrounding him, he instantly seized his rifle and fired, & sprang upon his horse, 10 or 12 shots were fired at him. the swiftness of his horse only saved him, it was late when he reached camp. He thinks the party might be about 20 men. Two others of the men Pichette and Aubichon,[9] cut across the point to the Eastward to the other fork of the river to set their traps, and have not yet arrived. they told some of the other men they meant to sleep out. I am nevertheless much alarmed for their safety, as the road they passed they were liable to be seen by these murdering Blackfeet, besides they are both men of little experience in the plains. It is too late to send in quest of them tonight.

Wedy 10. Fine weather. Did not raise camp today in order to allow the horses to feed and repose a little of which they are in much want. Notwithstanding the short days journies we make many of them are very lean, and the most of their hoofs so much worn with the stony road we have lately passed that they are becoming lame, some of them so much so that they can

[8] Antoine Hoole. He started with the 1831–32 expedition but became ill and was left at Fort Nez Perces in September, 1831.

[9] Baptiste Aubichon or Obichon. Both spellings are used in company records, though the latter seems more frequent. I have used the former in appendix A because Work used it consistently in this journal.

go no more a hunting until they get better. The men visited their traps but no more signs of beaver. 14 beaver were taken, which are few for the number of traps in the water. Sent Payette and five men to look after the two men who slept out last night. they met them coming home. They saw the fresh tracks of two horsem[en] but no Indians.

Thursdy 11. Constant heavy rain all day. In consequence of the bad weather we did not move camp. Though it rained in the valley it snowed in the Mountains & a considerable depth of snow seems to have fallen on the high grounds. Some Blackfeet were prowling about our camp in the night and kept us on the alert, it was so dark that they could not be discovered. Nor from the rain setting in before daylight could we ascertain from their tracks the probable number. they are supposed to be the same party that fired upon A. Hoole two days ago; they kept us on the alarm all night. Thus it is with us in this part of the country, when other people's labours cease and are succeeded by sleep and repose, Our troubles and anxiety begins. The apprehension of an attack in the light of day is bad enough but nothing compared to the dread of one in the night and perhaps too an overwhelming number.

Friday 12. Cloudy cold weather. Cut across the point about 10 miles N. E. to the North branch of the river.[10] The road broken and hilly and in places very slippery from the late rains. we encamped at a fine feeding place for the horses and a good situation for defense. The river here runs from S. E. to N. W. it is well wooded on its banks with poplar and willows, beyond which it is clear ground. the valley is but narrow. This stream is about the same size of the one we left. Blackfeet were *again about our camp last* night.

[10] The Lemhi River, not the stream now known as the North Fork.

45

Satdy 13. Snowed all day, in the valley the snow lies near half a foot deep, the depth on the mountains now must be considerable. We did not raise camp. Some of the men visited the traps six beaver were taken. they complain of a great scarcity of beaver considering the fine appearance of the river for them, and the numbers which were formerly found in it. Indians have been hunting here lately as well as in the other fork.

Sunday 14. Mild weather, but cold in the night. Did not raise camp. 10 beaver were taken. The river is getting frozen up so that the traps cant be set.

Mondy 15. Very cold in the night. Cloudy cold weather during the day. Proceeded up the river about 8 miles. the river here takes a turn to the S. E.[11] Only three beaver were taken this morning. Several of the men were out hunting and killed a few sheep.

Tuesdy 16. Froze keen in the night. Cloudy mild weather during the day. Did not raise camp today, in consequence of too much time being taken up in the morning pursuing a party of Blackfeet. They had been lurking about our camp in the night and approached quite close to the horses and lodges unperceived by the guard. their tracks were seen in the morning when a party went after them but they gained the mountain and could not be come up with. They are supposed to be about 20 in number, and are probably the same party that attacked A. Hoole a few days ago.

Shortly after this a party of Flat Heads arrived to pay us a visit. their camp is on the opposite side of the mountain to the Eastward,[12] about a days going off. Every one is glad to meet

[11] The party would be near the mouth of Haynes Creek.

[12] The Flatheads were probably camped on Prairie Creek, a branch of the Beaverhead River on the east side of Lemhi Pass. The pass was the usual route through the mountains here.

these people who are our real friends, what a difference between these people and the murderous Blackfeet though both Savages and inhabiting the same country. The Blackfeet short ago stole above 30 horses from the F Heads.

Wedy 17. Cloudy mild weather some light snow. Marched about 7 miles up the river S.E.[13] The snow is if any thing getting deeper as we advance. Some Buffalo bulls were seen and a herd of cows supposed to have been started from the Mountains by Blackfeet. A few more F. Heads headed by Old chief La Buche arrived. Three Nezperces also arrived in the evening their camp is on the opposite side of the Mountains some distance up. they separated from the F Heads some time ago, but are so much harrassed by the Blackfeet that they are glad to make their way back again. There are a few more lodges of Nezperces somewhere on the upper part of this river.

Thursdy 18. Cloudy rather mild weather. The snow wasted a little during the day, and the water in the river is rising which is a sign that the snow farther up is melting. Did not raise camp. The hunters see tracks of blackfeet in every direction. A party was encamped close too [*sic*] here short ago.

Friday 19. The weather soft and rather warm about noon. The snow wasted considerably. Took leave of our F Head friends in the morning and proceeded 10 miles up the river S. E. and encamped on a fine feeding point for the horses.[14] The road lay over some hills but was nevertheless good. The river is well wooded with poplar Alder and willow and has a fine appearance for beaver and some are still to be found in it but at present on account of the ice and the rising of the water it is difficult to take them. The hills begin to recede a little from

---

[13] Near the mouth of McDevitt Creek.
[14] This camp would be near the present site of Lemhi, Idaho.

the river. Some herds of buffaloe were seen, but only one was killed. We here found 5 lodges of Nezperces and F Heads one of the latter with his thigh broke. he met with misfortune in a battle with the Blackfeet some time ago.

Saturday 20. Cloudy mild weather. Did not raise camp, in order to allow the horses to feed. The people traded a few cords, appichimons[15] &c. from the Indians.

Sundy 21. Raw cold weather, blowing fresh. Proceeded 7 Miles up the river. The country bears the same appearance as these days past. Good feeding for the horses at our present encampment. Some of the hunters killed two or three buffaloe. these animals are very scarce though they used formerly to be very numerous in this quarter.

Monday 22. Blew a storm in the night, and stormy with snow showers during the day. Did not raise camp, Some of the people killed a few buffaloe, bulls.

Tuesdy 23. Raw cold weather, blowing fresh. Marched about 9 Miles E. S. E. up the river to a small poplar river which falls in from the Southward [Timber Creek]. The road good, here the river runs through a swamp, the small creeks frozen up.

Mr. Ogden passed part of the winter here some years ago, then there was neither ice nor snow in the valley. Formerly beaver were very numerous and there are still a few both in the main river & the streams that fall into it particularly the latter, but they cant be taken now on account of the ice.

[15] "Square pieces of robes, used under our saddles in travelling, or under our beds in camp" (Ferris, *Life in the Rocky Mountains*, 102). In the Columbia plateau region the word is pronounced "apishamore" and later came to mean a decorative throw to be placed behind the saddle.

It was very cold marching today, the women and children and some of the worst clothed men were nearly freezing. And even after encamping having to go some miles for wood it was some time before a fire was got to warm them. Formerly buffaloe used to be very numerous about this place, now scarcely one is to be seen, probably this arises from a party of Nezperces Indians having passed not long since and driven the buffaloe off to the great plain, where they have not yet returned there probably being little or no snow there.

A few Nezperces Indians accompany us from our last encampment, only four or five men of these people with their families proceeded down the river to follow the F Head camp, if they escape the Blackfeet it will be a wonder.

Wedy 24. Snowed all day and stormy toward evening. This fall together with the old snow make more than afoot deep of snow on the ground. On account of the bad weather, did not raise camp.

Thursdy 25. Blew a storm the forepart of the night very cold clear frosty weather during the day. Continued our route about 10 Miles up the river to the Fountain. This place was represented to me as never freezing, now scarcely as much water can be found unfrozen as will suffice the horses to drink, the swamp is also frozen so that the whole camp passed over it. As we ascend toward the height of land the snow becomes deeper. Two small rivers fall in from the North, and one from the South. Wood is so scarce that scarcely any thing but green poplar can be got to warm us cold as the weather is.

Friday 26. Overcast cold weather blowing fresh. Marched about 5 Miles up the little river which is here very small, and near its source [Eighteen Mile Creek]. A small stream falls in from the South. It was very cold for the women and children. The men went after buffalo and killed a few bulls, a large herd of cows were started near the Mountain, but none of them killed. The bull beef bad as it is is at present acceptable as provisions are getting scarce in the camp.

Saturday 27. Blew a storm in the night & very cold stormy and cold all day. It being too cold for the women and children we did not raise camp. No buffalo to be seen in our neighborhood.

Sunday 28. Raw cold weather, some light snow blowing fresh and drifting. Crossed the height of land about 12 Miles S. E.[16] The snow in places about 2 feet deep, the road occasionally hilly yet pretty good. The poorer horses were nevertheless pretty much fatigued, the most of the people were also ready to stop by the time we reached the camp, which is at a small creek where there is good feeding for the horses. A few buffaloe bulls were seen but no cows, one or two bulls were killed. The country we passed today has a dreary appearance.

Monday 29. Snowed the forepart of the day fine mild weather afterwards. The unfavourable weather in the morning prevented us from raising camp, it was too late to start after it became fine.

Tuesdy 30. Mild weather in the morning, cold & blowing with some snow in the afternoon. Marched 15 Miles S. E. to a little below what is called the fountain a kind of swamp whence a pretty large river rises.[17] The Mountains here ap-

---

[16] The height of land would be the divide between Eighteen Mile Creek and Mud Creek.

[17] The only large stream which could be meant would be Birch Creek, in which valley the party was then encamped. The camp would be near the present site of Reno, Idaho.

proach close to the river, but both above and below recede from it to a considerable extent. This was a hard days march both on horses and people, and unfortunately there is very little grass for the horses, and scarcely wood to warm the people cold as the weather is. Seven buffaloe were seen and the people went in pursuit of them, they turned out all to be bulls.

December, 1830

Wedy 1. Clear cold weather, blowing fresh. Proceeded about 8 miles S. S. E. from the river to a small creek at the foot of the mountains at the entrance of a pass which leads to Day's defile.[1] We are induced to take this road in preference to another road the South end of the mountain, as it is rather shorter and likely to yield better feeding for our horses. it is also expected that we will find buffaloe numerous in Days defile and make some provisions as we go on. Six of the men A. Finlay, P. Finlay, M. Finlay, A. Hoole, A Plante, & Bt. Gardipie[2] separated from the camp and took the other road round the end of the Mountains [Lemhi Range] with a few Nezperces Indians who were with us. These men are all half breeds and as whimsical as pure Indians with whom they [were] principally brought up. They sent one of their number to me to state their intention. I endeavoured to deter them from doing so but without effect. We will meet in a few days again at a

[1] Pass Creek. The creek that flows down the west face of the range opposite the head of Pass Creek is also called Pass Creek on all USC&GS maps. Mr. E. C. Phoenix of Pocatello, Idaho, lent me a Forest Service map which listed the west-flowing stream as Uncle Ike Creek. The Geodetic Survey, perhaps in good taste, does not recognize this name.

[2] Baptiste Gardipie. He was with Work again in 1831–32 and on the Bonaventura expedition of 1832–33.

place called Little Lake.[3] It would never do were I to follow the whims of every one relative to the road to take.

Thursdy 2. Clear fine weather. Crossed the Mountain a distance of 16 miles S. to Mr. McKenzies encampment in Day's defile.[4] The road through the pass though hilly and uneven is not bad yet on account of the length of the encampment and the depth of the snow about 3 feet on the height of land it was a hard day both on horses and people, both being much tired when we put up. There is as a recompense excellent feeding for the horses. One horse gave up on the way. There is but little snow in the defile. Sheep are very numerous in the mountain a few were killed. Some herds of buffaloe are to be seen in the valley below.

Friday 3. Some light snow, mild weather. Moved about 8 Miles S. to the little river in the middle of the valley where we stopped at a tolerably good feeding place for the horses.[5] The hunters at the same time went after buffaloe and killed several. Our last encampment affords better feeding for the horses than this one but being so close to the Mountain it was more unsafe, as Blackfeet might be in the vicinity without our knowledge.

Satdy 4. Light snow and thick fog all day. Did not raise

[3] Probably the sinks of the Little Lost River.

[4] Donald McKenzie. This entry is of interest to the devotees of the cult of the grave of John Day. A study of other accounts of this site leads me to the conclusion that Work's entry is misleading and should not be relied upon in attempting to fix the site of Day's grave. This is in direct contradiction to my earlier, published view ("The Lost River of John Day," *Idaho Yesterdays*, II [1959], 6–10). The unpublished Alexander Ross journal of 1824 seems to me to be the only reliable source. See B 202/a/1, June 1, 1824.

[5] The Little Lost River below the mouth of Pass Creek (Uncle Ike Creek).

camp. The weather being unfavourable for hunting none of the people went in pursuit of buffaloe but they were busily employed curing the meat that was killed yesterday, & making appichimons cords &c.

Sunday 5. Mild weather, but snowed all day. Did not raise camp. Several of the people went a hunting but no buffaloe were to be seen, but from the darkness of the weather they could not see to any great distance. Though it snowed all day the fall of snow is but light.

Mondy 6. Clear cold weather. Did not raise camp. Several of the people went a hunting but no buffaloe were to be found in the Plains. C Plante killed 4 in the mountain.

Tuesdy 7. Light snow most of the day. The unfavourable weather deterred us from raising camp. No buffalo to be seen.

Wdy 8. Cloudy mild weather, some light snow.
Marched 7 Miles S. E. by E. down the river to a clump of poplar. The road good, but no grass for the horses so that they have nothing but small wormwood and not much even of that. In the morning some small bands of buffaloe were observed descending from the mountains. the people went in pursuit and killed 12 of them. Some large herds were seen from the camp late in the evening but it was too late to pursue them.

Thursdy 9. Stormy weather, Snow and drifting. Continued our journey S. E. 9 Miles down the river to where it terminates in a small lake or swamp, and thence 8 miles across the plains to a dry branch of Goddin's river.[6] here we found good

---

[6] The small lake or swamp would be the sinks of the Little Lost River. The dry branch of Goddin's river would be the main stream of Big Lost River near the sinks of that stream.

feeding for the horses and the only place any was to be found since our last camp but no water, this channel which is now dry is scarcely fordable in the spring and early part of the summer. There are a few poplar and willows on its banks. The snow here is more than a foot deep but very soft so that it appears to be not long since it fell.

Large herds of buffaloe were seen in the evening but it was too late to go in pursuit of them from their tracks they appear to be numerous in the plains. Antelopes are also seen in large herds.

Friday 10. Clear cold weather. Did not raise camp in order to allow the horses to feed and repose after their hard day's march yesterday. No buffaloe to be seen near our camp. The party who separated from us on the 1st Inst. came up with us today. They saw the tracks of several parties of Blackfeet, and found a horse left by them. The excuse these men make for their going off is that they supposed the other road better for their horses which they apprehended would have been too weak to cross the Mountain. They lost some of their horses (4) which gave up from fatigue by the way.

Satdy 11. Froze keen in the night, clear cold weather during the day. Continued our route across the plains about 10 miles S. E. where we put up for the night with only wormwood to warm us and what is worse very little grass for our horses. The road pretty good but in places stony. The snow a little more than a foot deep and very loose. The country covered with wormwood. Two lean broke down horses gave up by the way and could not be got on. The snow in places completely trod down by the buffaloe which are passing backwards & forwards in large herds.

Sundy 12. Foggy cold weather, an exceedingly bitter cold

55

night. Proceeded on our journey to the Middle Bute[7] 10 Miles S. E. The Snow near 1½ foot deep. The country still covered with wormwood, as we approach the Bute the grass becomes more abundant among the wormwood, here the horses will find a good deal of food. There are also some stunted cedars around the Bute which yields fuel. About forty of the horses passed the guard in the night and returned to the last encampment, it was late by the time they were got back. 18 of the poorer horses gave up by the way, some of them scarcely fit to leave the encampment, the piercing cold in the night where there was no shelter so benumbed them that they could scarcely stir. One of the Companie's mules was dead in the morning. Numerous large herds of buffalo were seen during the day. but from the helpless state of the horses none of them were pursued.

Monday 13. Foggy part of the day. The weather still cold but milder than these days past. Did not raise camp in order to allow the horses to feed and repose, and to endeavour to bring up those that were left yesterday, some of which were brought to the camp. 7 were found dead and some could not be found supposed to have returned to the last encampment or the one before. The most of these horses were so broke down and so lean that they could not stand cold.

Tuesdy 14. Foggy cold weather. Proceeded across the little height of land to the end of the Cedars about 7 Miles S. E. here we found a good deal of grass for the horses but the depth of the snow prevents them from feeding well. One or two more of the horses gave up on the way. A herd of many hundred elk

---

[7] The western of the twin buttes located in the Snake River plains. The buttes were a noted landmark in Oregon Trail times as well as being the normal stopping place for fur trade parties crossing the plains on the north-south route.

was started near our camp they were pursued and 25 killed notwithstanding the poverty of the horses. Buffaloe were also seen in different directions in the plain below.

Wedy 15. Very dense fog the greater part of the day so much so that until towards evening nothing could be seen at any distance. The weather milder than these days past, the snow thawing a little towards evening. Continued our journey across the plain 9 Miles S. E. The snow begins to diminish a little, the country still maintains the same appearance except one portion of the plain which we passed which is clear of wormwood and has some coarse grass peeping through the snow. Encamped in a little clump of cedar. There is some grass *among the wormwood* for the horses but it is buried under snow and difficult for the horses to get at in their weak state.

Thursdy 16. Cloudy mild weather. Snow thawed a little in the night and during the day. Stormy in the night. The snow diminished a good deal. Marched 7 Miles S. E. where we put up as it would have been too long to gain the river. The country still bears the same appearance. Two horses died last night and some more jaded during the day, one was lost and could not be found in the morning. Only wormwood to warm us with in the night. Some buffaloe were seen and the tracks of numerous herds crossed our road these two days past.

Friday 17. Stormy in the night and during the day, thawing *with sleet showers towards evening.*
   Arrived at Snake river at *Blackfoot hill*[8] late in the evening, where we have the pleasure of finding good feeding for the horses though there is a good deal of snow on the ground. Probably owing to the change in the weather the horses strayed off to a great distance in the night and it was late in the day before

[8] Ferry Butte, near Blackfoot, Idaho.

they were all found. a band of them had strayed off farther than the others and were found by a party of Snakes who were hunting who immediately brought them to our people who were in quest of them and assisted in finding some more that were missing. We had kept no guard since we arrived at the Bute as confining the horses in the night would have killed them. A great many Snake Indians are encamped round us in their Camps two below and one above. they complain that few buffaloe are to be found near. The river here is partially frozen over at places. It is here about 60 yards wide and runs from S. E. to N. W. there is a good ford at this place.

Satdy 18. Rather cold weather some snow and sleet.

The people brought up some horses which became fatigued on the road yesterday. The loss of horses altogether crossing the plain amounts to 26 and unfortunately the loss falls heaviest on the poorest individuals of our community who are worst able to bear it. It was the severe cold which caused the loss. had the weather been milder, notwithstanding the snow very few of the horses would have been lost. Different parties have passed at a much later season than this.

Several Snake Indians and one of their Chiefs visited us to-day. There are a great many of these people encamped here within a short distance of us. No Blackfeet have been seen here for some [time] till today when a party were observed near the mountains two of whom the Snakes killed and scalped.

Sundy 19. Mild thawing weather. This mild weather is of infinite advantage to our horses. Some more Snakes visited us, gave a triffling present to three of the principal chiefs. Some more Blackfeet were seen in the mountain by the Snake Scouts. This induces to keep guard on the horses in the night as well as day. A party of the Snakes passed in the morning bearing in triumph the scalps and portions of the mangled members of the two Blackfeet they killed yesterday. And the day has been passed among them celebrating a war dance.

Monday 20. Fine mild weather. Still several Indians visiting us. The people are trading leather and some other articles which they require from them. Some of the people have yet gone to seek after buffaloe, though provisions are scarce with us. It is necessary to allow the horses to repose a little. Some of the men set a few traps for beaver. The Americans were hunting about this quarter in the summer & fall. it is only a few days since a party of them crossed the mountain to White river in the neighbourhood of which they are to winter.[9]

We found the late P. L'Etang's rifle[10] with one of the Snake Indians. he found it in some bushes. it is supposed the murdering Blackfoot who possessed himself of it had fallen sick and had been left by his party. the marks of several places where he had been lying was observed about the place, his bow and arrows were also left.

Tuesdy 21. Clear rather cold weather. A large body of the Snakes paid us a visit on horseback & as a mark of friendship made three turns round our camp, firing volleys as they passed round. they were all armed and had the scalps and mangled members of the two Blackfeet, which they killed a few days ago, suspended from their horses' bridles. the chief men got to smoke, & a trifling present was made to two or three of the chiefs. A party of our men went to hunt, and found a herd of buffalo not far off but just as they fell in with them they heard the firing of the Snake Indians at our camp and imagining it was

---

[9] This party is unidentified but is not one of the two parties of Americans previously mentioned. A further mention of the party and a clue to the location of White River is to be found in the entry for January 2, 1831, and note below.

[10] Pierre L'Etang, whose rifle was lost when he was killed by the Blackfeet, see September 25 above.

an attack of the Blackfeet they left the buffalo and made the best of their way home as fast as their horses could carry them.

Wedy 22. Cloudy mild weather, some snow towards evening. A party of the people went a hunting and killed 12 buffalo on the opposite side of the river.

Thursdy 23. Cloudy soft weather Snow thawing. Some of the hunters were out and killed a large beaver, the others who had traps set caught none.

Friday 24. Snowing & blowing fresh all day, cold towards evening. In consequence of the coldness of the weather and the poverty of our horses they were driven into the woods and the night watch dispensed with, by confining them in the night they cannot feed and the poorer ones run a risk of dieing with the cold. It is the opinion of the more experienced of the people that on account of the depth of the snow on the ground the Blackfeet are not likely to be stirring about much now. From our neighbours the Snakes we apprehend no danger as we are on good terms with them.

Satdy 25. Clear fine weather. About ½ foot of snow fell yesterday and last night. There is a little more than a foot deep of snow on the ground.

Sundy 26. Cloudy mild weather the snow thawing. Some of the people were off hunting and killed 10 buffaloe.

Mondy 27. Stormy in the night and blowing fresh all day, and the snow thawing fast. This mild weather is of infinite advantage to our weak lean horses.

Tuesdy 28. Stormy with rain most of the night and stormy

during the day. The snow dropping rapidly. Several spots in the plain bare. Some of the hunters were out and killed one buffalo.

Wedy 29. Froze a little in the night. Overcast light snow the greater part of the day. The unfavourable weather prevented the people from going a hunting.

Thursdy 30. Cloudy cold weather. The people went a hunting, & fell in with a large herd of buffalo but they fled to the mountains where the snow was so deep that they could not be pursued with horses, and none were killed.

Friday 31. Blew a storm in the night, and stormy with snow all day, but not cold.

January, 1831

Satdy 1. Clear mild weather. This being Newyears day none of the people went a hunting, they endeavoured to regale themselves the best way they could though many of them had no fresh meat in consequence of their not falling in with buffaloe two days ago. Each man was treated with a dram and some cakes in the morning.

Sundy 2. Fog and light snow the greater part of the day. The unfavourable weather deterred the people from going a hunting. Late last night a party of 16 Nezperces and Flatheads arrived from the American camp at White river on the east side of the mountains.[1] they have been ten days on the journey, they walked on snow shoes, the snow on the mountain is very deep. These people sold their horses to the American freemen and obtained very high prices for them. they have a great many blankets, scarlet, green, blue & white and *fine* cloth scarlet & blue, besides a variety of other articles. They are the bearers of presents to the Nezperces and Flat Head chiefs, and bring word the Americans are to pass this way next spring to trade with the F Heads and form an establishment on their lands.

---

[1] If the direction and distance of travel are correct, the American party would have been wintering in the Beaverhead country and could not have been one of the American parties previously mentioned in the journal. White River is a name that eludes identification.

The Americans represent themselves as consisting of two parties, One Americans and one of people like us. There are six chiefs and a great many men.[2]

Mondy 3. Overcast some snow in the evening. A great many of the people were hunting & killed 16 buffaloe. they saw several large herds, except near the river the snow is deep and very hard so that it is very fatiguing on the horses to run the buffaloe, indeed it requires a good horse to catch one now. The Snake Indians stole a horse from Champaigne. it is a horse which was changed with them at the crossing place below, and is said to have been stolen by the man who changed him. it is said to be his rightful owner or some of his relations that has taken him now. The chiefs have been spoke to to warn him, they all deny that it is any of their people that took him, but a band of scoundrels that are below.

Tuesdy 4. Thick fog & rimy weather light snow the most of the day. Two of the people went a hunting, & killed 2 buffaloe. the weather was unfavourable for the chase.

Wedy 5. The weather as yesterday snowing the most of the day. Though the snow is light the quantity on the ground is accumulating, these two days about 5 inches in depth has fallen. The Indians stole another horse, this one was also obtained from them in exchange for another one below. These exchanges with the Indians are always attended with trouble, for if they find the horse they get becomes poor or dies, or that they have not made a good bargain, They will endeavour to take back their own horse again. The Chief has been spoke to and made to understand that stealing our horses will be productive of a

[2] No trading post was, in fact, established, but American parties did hunt through this area and north to the Flathead country in 1831. Work was to meet American trappers in the Flathead country in 1832.

quarrel. he promised to use his influence to get the horses back, and sent off immediately for the purpose. The Indians assembled here are of different tribes of the Snakes and from different quarters and many of them belong to no chief and are such wanderers that when they commit a crime by stealing a horse there is no knowing where to find them. We must run the risk of having some of our horses stolen as it is out of our power to prevent it except by keeping guard over the horses in the night as well as in the day, and by confining the horses in the night with the quantity of snow that is now on the ground & the state of the weather numbers of them would inevitably die.

Thursdy 6. Cloudy weather, Milder than these days past the sun faintly appeared for the first time these several days. The wind also changed from the N. to the S.W. An Indian came crying to the camp in the evening. it was ascertained after some time that some of his countrymen from a lower camp had stolen five of the horses.

Friday 7. Overcast some light snow mixed with rain. The snow thawing a little. On account of the unfavourable weather none of the people went a hunting.

Satdy 8. Overcast dark weather. A buffaloe was killed among the horses & gored one of them.

Sundy 9. Cloudy cold weather. The coldness of the weather prevented the people from going a hunting.

Mondy 10. Fine clear mild weather. Several of the people went a hunting, but unfortunately the Indians had raised the buffaloe before they arrived so that only three or four buffaloe were killed, one of which furiously turned upon the hunter and gored the horse in the flank so severely that it is to be apprehended he will die. The horses were fatigued today to little purpose, which they could ill bear as the most of them are very lean and though they have still some grass yet it is of such a quality that they are not likely to fatten upon it even when they are doing nothing, but less when they are worked. I have been some time waiting for a favourable day to move a little farther down the river where it is said there is better feeding for the horses; but wished the people to have some fresh meat to serve them a few days as we may not immediately find buffaloe below on account of Indians being encamped in different directions around us. There is a good place for encamping a little above on the opposite side of the river and near buffaloe; but though experienced hands tell me that there is now no danger of the Blackfeet on account of the depth of snow yet I am unwilling to run the risk and would willingly be so situated that a camp of the Snakes would be above us so that should the Blackfeet come they might receive the first visit.

Tuesdy 11. Fine warm weather. Raised camp & moved about 10 miles down the river to a place called the little house. there is good feeding for the horses but the snow is still near a foot deep, which is nearly the same as where we left. Firewood is rather scarce. We intended to have encamped a little farther down but the place is occupied by the Indians. The F. Head and Nezperces Indians who arrived on the 1st Inst left us for their own lands. I wrote by them to the gentlemen & Colvile[3] & Vancouver.

Wedy 12. Raw cold, foggy, rimy weather. The most of the

---

[3] Fort Colville was located near Kettle Falls, Washington, at a site chosen by Governor George Simpson in 1825. John Work had been in charge of much of the construction of the post and had been employed there prior to his being assigned to the command of the Snake Country brigade. The post was named for Andrew Colvile, then a director of the Hudson's Bay Company.

Indians whom we left above are passing down to below us so that we will still be the first to meet the Blackfeet should they come, however we will be the first to find the buffaloe if as is expected they descend along the river when there are no Indians to disturb & drive them back.

Thursdy 13. Cloudy cold weather. A party of six men and an Indian went off to hunt buffaloe above our old encampment. Some more of the Indians moving down from above, few remain there now.

Friday 14. Very cold in the night, & clear cold weather all day. One of our horses is missing but whether stolen or strayed is not known. he is a very small lean horse.

Satdy 15. Weather as yesterday. Three more horses all weak lean horses were stolen by the Indians last night, but in what direction they are taken we cannot yet ascertain. Reports are in circulation that the Indians mean to take some of our horses to pay for some of their people who were killed by the trappers on Ogden's and Sandwich island rivers two years ago,[4] and that the Caiuses and Nezperces who are with us have been told to put their horses apart from ours so that they may not be taken. It is considered that little reliance may be placed on these reports as they had it in their power to take vengeance on a small party of only 8 of our men last winter had they chosen.

Sunday 16. Still clear & in the night piercing cold weather, however the sun is powerful in the height of the day and melts some of the snow in places facing Southwards. This cold weather is severe on our lean weak horses.

[4] Sandwich Island River was, of course, the Owyhee River, as Captain James Cook had named the Hawaiian Islands the Sandwich Islands. I find no mention of such an incident in surviving journals, but the 1829–30 journal was lost in a canoe accident at The Dalles.

Mondy 17. Weather continues still the same. We were alarmed last night by a war whoop on the other side of the river opposite our camp and considered it as coming from some Snakes who had been alarmed by Blackfeet, but afterwards ascertained that it was only a cry of a young man who had been at a gambling party. We had some intelligence of our horses, and an Indian the little Nezperces[5] is engaged to accompany some of the men in quest of them. They are taken by a party that is departing down the river and which bears the character of great rascals, which with justice may be applied to the greater part of the Indians by whom we are surrounded.

Tuesdy 18. Weather the same. The three men who started yesterday with the Little Nezperces returned with the four horses that were last stolen, they found them at the American rapid[6] below the river Bannack [Bannock Creek] and had some trouble getting them. Our hunters also arrived from above, they have made no great chase for the length of time they have been absent.

Wedy 19. Clear frosty weather very cold in the night and the morning. The sun warm in the middle of the day. Some of the people went a hunting and killed some buffaloe but they were very lean. A horse *J. Despard's* was stolen yesterday or the night before we have been able to get no intelligence of him as yet. It is conjectured he is taken by some of the scamps from whom the horses were taken on the 18th.

Thursdy 20. Raw cold weather, clear & very cold in the night and morning. Some of the men who killed the buffaloe yesterday brought home the meat.

---

[5] This is the first mention of "The Little Nezperces," whose name is never given. He was obviously a superior tracker.
[6] American Falls of the Snake River.

Friday 21. Clear weather, very cold in the morning, but milder afterwards than these days past. A party of the men went to hunt buffaloe, two of them returned in the evening with a fine fat cow, the others intend to sleep out one or two nights and endeavour to kill the buffaloe afoot, as running them with horses is very fatiguing on the horses in their present weak state, and the depth of snow nearly a foot deep, on the ground, the most of which is very hard crusted, and very difficult to run in. Buffaloe are very numerous at Blackfoot hill.

I had intended to raise camp and move a little farther down the river to a situation where grass would be more plentiful near the camp than here so that we might commence keeping guard over the horses immediately, but considering that while the weather continues so cold and so much snow on the ground confining the horses at night would cause the death of a great many of them, I changed the plan & risk them a little longer. Moreover here we are in the neighbourhood of the best of the Indians & they tell us that the most of the scamps who would be most likely to steal have moved down the river. The scarcity of meat also rendered it necessary to not omit the opportunity of getting a supply of the buffaloe that are now about Blackfoot hill. In the evening 8 or 10 Indians arrived from below, and traded 5 or 6 beaver, a sort of a chief among them, who is known to several of the men & represented as a good Indian, expresses himself indignant at the Indians stealing our horses and states we may be under no apprehension of any of his people taking any of them. The day before yesterday two Caiouse Indians & two young men who accompanied us from the Fort left to go home, & when going off one of them chief Allicat's brother went to the plain & without ceremony took one of Quintall's[7] horses, the horsekeeper was so stupid as to allow him to go

---

[7] Laurent Quintall. He had been with the 1824–25 expedition and was one of those who stood by Ogden in the scuffle with the deserters (*HBRS*, XIII, 234).

John Work

Mrs. John Work, née Josette Legacé

Peter Skene Ogden

Old Fort Walla Walla, commonly called Fort Nez Perces,
built in 1818 by Donald Mackenzie and the point from which
Work's expedition departed.

Little Lost River, Day's Defile, showing the sinks in the foreground.

Little Lost River and Pass Creek, the site of Work's winter camp.

Steens Mountain, southeastern Oregon, overlooking the
Alvord Valley.

View from summit of Steens Mountain over the Alvord Valley.

The Steens Mountains overshadowing Mann Lake.

Oregon State Highway Commission

of[f] with him. Quintall and Toupin[8] to interpret for him followed to his camp in the evening, but could not recover the horse, the reason the Indian assigned for taking him was because one of his men got a beating from some of the men when he took a gun to shoot some time ago. The other Indians advised the men not to attempt taking the horse by force lest he would shoot him but to return in the morning & they would endeavour to persuade him in the night to give him up quietly. Quintall returned and only took an Indian with him instead of 3 or 4 men as I advised, and when the scoundrel saw him alone he would not return the horse, but gave another one. Indians with the camp are a nuisance, these scoundrels had their horses taken care of with the men's horses ever since they left the fort, and this is the reward they give now. Our horses are too lean and weak to pursue them.

Satdy 22. Light clouds fine mild weather, it is to be hoped good weather is going to set in now and there is much need for it on account of our horses. Champaigne traded a horse from the chief of the Indians that arrived yesterday, it turned out afterwards that he had stole the horse on his way here and the proper owner came in pursuit of him, so much for his professed abhorrence of theft.

Sundy 23. Cold in the morning fine Mild weather during the day. Rocques horse was stolen yesterday morning, he had been off for meat and ran away, the Indians that stole him found him by the way and took him off. Some of the people that were off hunting returned with very little meat, though they saw a great many buffaloe, but from some mismanagement they killed very few.

[8] Jean Baptiste Toupin. He had been the interpreter at Fort Nez Perces for several years but had joined the Snake Country brigade in 1829 and was to be with Work again in 1831–32.

Mondy 24. Cloudy fine mild weather. The horse that was missing yesterday was found by the assistance of an Indian. The rest of the people who were off hunting arrived without meat. A party of five more men started to hunt buffaloe which are said to be very numerous along the foot of the Mountain opposite to us.

Tuesdy 25. Foggy cold weather in the morning, fine weather afterwards. A number more of the people went off to hunt buffaloe, and two of those who went off yesterday returned late in the evening with the meat of two cows. They represent the buffaloe as being very numerous, and great numbers of Indians as well as our people in pursuit of them. The Indians are both on horse back and afoot the greater part afoot, if they find a buffaloe dead no matter by whom killed or what mark is left upon it, they cut it up immediately and carry it off as if it was their own, but if the proper owner comes at the time they relinquish it at once. One of the men caught a beaver yesterday. Some traps were set but on account of the intense cold weather the beavers do not stir out and the waters are frozen up. There are a few beaver, but they are very shy. This neighbourhood was hunted by the Americans last summer and fall.

Wedy 26. Thick fog in the morning, Cloudy mild weather afterwards. Some more of the people who were off hunting returned with meat. They bring the news that Payette who started yesterday with some youths to hunt, lost all his horses last night and had not yet found them. they are 8 in number and supposed to have strayed off. Or perhaps gone off with a herd of buffaloe.

Thursdy 27. Light snow the forepart of the day. Mild weather.

The boy Peerish[9] and two Indian youths who were with Payette arrived afoot. they had been seeking the strayed horses yesterday but could not find them. they are not supposed to be stolen as no Indian tracks were seen about Blackfoot river[10] where they are encamped. The Indians report that Blackfeet are seen in the mountains close to here.

Some Snake Indians stole or rather without leave borrowed three of our horses *last night or this morning* to make a trip to the foot of the mountain for meat. Another Indian one of our friends met and took them from them who had taken them away, arrived with them late in the evening much jaded. he was rewarded for his trouble.

Friday 28. Some light snow in the morning, Mild weather afterwards. Sent off Peerish and Pichette to seek after the strayed horses about Blackfoot river where they were lost. Two others Kanotta & Birnie[11] made a turn around the Indian's camps and through the plains also in quest of the horses and returned in the evening without any intelligence of them. The Indian chiefs are to send their people in quest of them. Several of the people who were off hunting arrived loaded with meat. More reports of Blackfeet being seen in the Mountains by the Indians. Should they descend the Snakes are encamped between them and us so that we are in little danger from them. The most of the Natives who were encamped near us here have removed to towards the mountains, where they will be nearer the buffaloe, they will also be nearer the enemy.

Satdy 29. Some light snow in the morning, Mild weather

[9] Boy Peerish is the only known name for this lad. He was probably the son of Pierre Martineau, sometimes known as Peerish.

[10] Blackfoot River is a tributary of the Snake River. The mouth of the stream is near the present community of Blackfoot, Idaho.

[11] P. Birnie. He was with Work again in 1831–32 and 1832–33 with the Bonaventura brigade.

afterwards. In the evening Payette & the people I sent off yesterday to seek the horses, arrived loaded with meat, but no news of the horses. indeed they scarcely looked after them, which is strange conduct and the reason they assign for it is that is a supposition that the Indians have found them. An Indian arrived in the evening with one of them states he found him with two others, which he will bring tomorrow, in the plains but did not see any thing of the other five.

Sundy 30. Raw foggy weather in the morning. Sent off six men to seek the stray horses. They made a turn of the Indian camps and having no intelligence of them did not go further in quest of them.

Mondy 31. Unpleasant weather, Snowed most of the day. The unfavourable weather deterred me from sending people off in quest of the lost horses. Several of the men who lately returned from the hunting excursion are afflicted with sore eyes occasioned by the snow. The Indian brought the other two horses. A party of six Indians arrived on horseback from below, they report that there are plenty of buffaloe at the American falls, and not much snow.

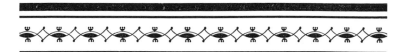

February, 1831

Tuesdy 1. Snowed in the night and all day, the weather warm and the snow nearly melting as it falls. This weather is very unfavourable for our lean horses. The Indians who arrived yesterday departed on their return today.

Wedy 2. The weather cleared up a little in the morning but afterwards snowed with a fresh breeze and cold the most of the day. Five men went to seek the lost horses. Four men also went to hunt buffaloe.

Thursdy 3. Raw cold weather, Some light snow in the morning. Near a foot deep of snow has fallen these few days past. The quantity of snow on the ground and the cold weather Is much against our weak horses. Two of the men who went in quest of the lost horses returned, without having seen any thing of them. Some of the hunters arrived near midnight last night with meat.

Friday 4. Overcast mild weather, some light snow.
The rest of the men who were in quest of the lost horses returned unsuccessful. On account of the late snow no vestiges of them can be seen. The rest of the people who were off hunting also returned with meat.

73

Satdy 5. Cloudy cold weather. Some light snow in the morning.

An Indian arrived from the camp and stated that our lost horses were there and that he had seen three of them. he was offered a reward if he would bring them, or take us to where they were, which he promised to do.

Sundy 6. Disagreeable raw cold foggy rimy weather.

Sent Payette and Kannota to the Indian camp to look after and gain information of our lost horses. No inteligence could be obtained of them, the lame chief, is off seeking after them. it is suspected they are among the Indians, and that they conceal them. An Indian arrived from Raft river, he represents the snow as being deeper there than even here, and that though there are some buffaloe, the Indians are starving as their horses are not able to catch them.

Mondy 7. Clear weather mild in the morning, but blowing fresh and very cold afterwards. Moved camp a few miles up the river to a place where grass was said to be plentiful, and where the horses can be kept nearer the camp, and wood for fuel got with less difficulty than the place we left. Instead of coming up the river I intended to have moved downwards a little but was deterred from doing so by being told that the grass had been burnt in the fall by the Indians. In our present situation we are a little nearer the buffaloe which is of some advantage to our horses in their weak state. The children and some of the grown people were nearly benumbed with the cold by the time we encamped.

the lame chief paid us a visit, he says he has been able to obtain no information regarding our lost horses. The Indian who arrived yesterday has a horse which was stolen from the F. Heads in the fall, but not by him. Some F Heads that are with us took him from him. I felt it necessary tho with reluctance to make them give him back, to prevent the Indians from stealing our horses in his place, and perhaps to deter them from returning those of ours that are supposed to be among them.

Tuesdy 8. A bitter cold night and very clear cold weather all day. The very cold weather deterred the people from going after buffaloe. Sent again to the camp to enquire after the lost horses, but the Little Nezperces who was applied to had heard nothing of them though he and a party had been seeking after them three days.

Wedy 9. Clear very cold weather in the night and during the day, but rather milder than yesterday. This cold weather is severe on our lean horses, one is nearly dead this morning, 3 died at our last camp. A party of the people went to hunt buffaloe. Some of them returned late at night with meat. They saw a good many buffaloe.

Thursdy 10. Clear very cold weather. Late last night five Indians arrived and said they had been seeking our stray horses but could not find them.

Friday 11. Cloudy weather milder than these days past.
Some of the people went a hunting on the opposite side of the river and killed three buffaloe but they were so lean that they did not think them worth bringing home.

Satdy 12. Cloudy fine mild weather. Some of the hunters who started on the 9th returned with meat. They also found two of the horses which were lost some time ago, not far from the place where they were lost, the poor animals are nearly dead with hunger, about that neighbourhood the grass is totally eaten up by the buffaloe.

Sundy 13. Mild weather, blowing fresh some snow in the morning. The rest of the people who were off hunting returned with meat. The buffaloe are in general very lean. Only a chance one to be found now a little fat. Some Elk that they killed are in better order. The unfavourable weather prevented me from sending off some people to seek the other three stray horses where the two were found yesterday.

Mondy 14. Some light snow in the morning, fine weather afterwards. Sent five men Kanota, Bernie, Quintall, Aubichon & Peerish to seek the stray horses. Six more of the men also went to hunt buffaloe, shortly afterwards the news arrived that they fell upon a track of a party of Blackfeet Indians with a band of the Snake Indians horses which they had stolen in the night or early in the morning and had gone in pursuit of them. Some of the poor Snakes had also gone after them.

Tuesdy 15. Cloudy cold weather, very keen frost and piercing cold in the night. The men who went in quest of the lost horses yesterday arrived in the evening with them, the poor animals are nearly starved to death and reduced to skin and bones with hunger and thirst. they were found in the plains not very far from where they were lost. These five men and M. Plant pursued the Blackfeet all day yesterday and came up with them near sunsetting on the opposite side of the river, the Indians abandoned the horses, 12 in number, and fled into the rocks where the people did not deem it prudent to pursue them, though they had every inclination to kill them had it been in their power. they brought back the horses and gave them to the chief the Horn[1] and one of his men who only reached the camp in the night, & from whom they had been stolen, he was

---

[1] Ferris speaks very highly of the Horn Chief and calls him the principal chief of the Snakes. He was killed by the Blackfeet in 1832 (Ferris, *Life in the Rocky Mountains*, 61, 149–50).

thankful for the service rendered. From the tracks, it is judged there were only four Blackfeet, they came from the Mountain opposite us and are supposed to be the residue or part of the band of whom the Snakes killed two when we arrived on the river,[2] and have passed the winter in the mountains until now when they made an attempt to escape with a few horses. The ones they took were from the Horn's camp which is nearest the mountain. the horses were entirely ill chosen for they are so miserably lean that they could have been scarcely taken two days march even had they not been pursued. It is not expected that those or any others will visit us again for some time as on account of the quantity of snow they would have little chance of escaping. Had these been pursued a little sooner or at a quicker pace they would have been overtaken in the plain, and not one of them would have escaped.

Wedy 16. Cold in the night, & cloudy cold weather during the day. The people who were off hunting arrived loaded with meat, the buffaloe are become very lean, but some Elk were killed which are still in pretty good order. The same Snake Chief & a party of his people paid us a visit, with some small articles to trade. The Chief says he intends shortly to come and encamp with us. Some of the people have some traps set for beaver. Longtain took two and Quintall one these two days past. There are a few beaver about this neighbourhood notwithstanding its having been so frequently hunted, but they are very shy and but few of the little rivers not frozen.

Thursdy 17. Cloudy mild weather. A party of the people went to hunt buffaloe and returned late in the evening loaded with meat, buffaloe are plentiful not far off. My Coille horse[3] was stolen by some scoundrel of an Indian last night or this

[2] See December 18 above.
[3] Evidently the horse's name.

morning. The lame chief who is encamped with us immediately sent off one of his young men in quest of him. Majeau[4] whom I sent with two mules for meat left one of them by the way, and he will probably be lost.

Friday 18. Overcast mild weather, some light snow & sleet, the snow thawing. Our friend the Little Nezperces arrived in the morning with the mule which was lost yesterday and informed us that my horse which was stolen yesterday morning was at the Indian camp, three men were sent with the Indian for him. the Indians it seems had not stolen but in their way borrowed him and run him after buffaloe all day yesterday. The Snakes have recently seen more Blackfeet in the mountain opposite to us, should they venture to descend they will meet with the Snakes before they come our length.

Satdy 19. Overcast dark weather some light snow in the morning, the snow thawing a little. I intended to raise camp today and move a little farther down the river where the horses will find better feeding and be near us, but was deterred from doing so by the unfavourable appearance of the weather.

Sundy 20. Some light snow in the night. Overcast soft weather during the day, the snow wasting considerably. Two of the young men who went to hunt elk yesterday returned, they killed 11 principally for the skins. We had a visit from some Snake Indians it seems they are holding a council to assemble in one body and encamp near us which they think will be the safest situation from the inroads of the Blackfeet, who are now beginning to move about.

Mondy 21. Light clouds, fine weather. Raised camp & moved

---

[4] A. Majeau. He was with Work again in 1831–32 and 1832–33. He had served a number of years with the company.

6 or 8 miles farther down the river where we will be enabled to keep our horses grazing nearer the camp than at our last camp. The snow is in general near a foot & a half deep and in many places much more and very fatiguing on the horses. It is also a work of no small labour clearing an encampment. At our present station there seems to be pretty good feeding for the horses, there is still better on the opposite side of the plain but we cannot go there at present on account of the want of wood for fuel.

Tuesdy 22. Keen frost in the night, raw cold weather in the morning, overcast and thawing a little afterwards.

Some of the people visited some traps they have set, two beaver were taken. The river is frozen so that in several situations where there are appearance of beaver traps cannot be set.

Wedy 23. Blew a storm with sleet and snow the greater part of the day. The snow is getting almost in water. One of the horses died, from the severity of the weather. Pichette caught an otter, and Dumais[5] a beaver.

Thursdy 24. Overcast, thawing, the snow wasting fast.

Nothing was found in the traps today. All about here was hunted by the Americans last summer and fall and what few beaver are left are very shy and difficult to take.

Friday 25. Some snow and sleet part of the day. Four of the people went to hunt buffalo, two of whom *Payette & Quintall* returned with loads of meat in the evening, the buffalo are now very lean, indeed they can scarcely be otherwise continually hunted and very little to eat. The snow still lies deep on the ground and is very heavy and very fatiguing on the horses to walk through it.

[5] A. Dumais. He was with Work again in 1831–32 and was drowned in the Snake River on July 19, 1832.

Satdy 26. Cloudy weather, froze a little in the night, which made a crust on the snow and renders feeding for the horses more difficult. thawed very little during the day. The ice in the river broke up opposite our camp.

The people visited their traps, and set some more, three beaver and an otter were taken. Pichette lost one of his traps.

Sundy 27. Cloudy weather some light snow. blowing fresh part of the day. The rest of the hunters who were off returned loaded with buffalo and elk meat all very lean. Two beaver were taken.

Mondy 28. Mild in the morning with light snow, but stormy with snow and sleet afterwards. This weather is very unfavourable for our lean weak horses, the snow is accumulating and not only very heavy but becoming crusted which renders it very difficult for the horses to find the grass. A party of the people went to hunt elk principally for the skins to make lodges of.

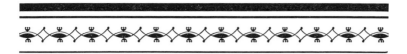

March, 1831

Tuesdy 1. Raw cold weather in the morning, stormy and some light snow during the day. Some of the people who went off yesterday returned with elk meat and skins. 1 Beaver was taken. The ice in the main river is only broke up in places and even then a portion still remains along the edges of the river so that it is only in some places a trap can be set.

Wedy 2. Blew a storm with snow and sleet all day, and the snow drifting so violently that one could scarcely look out. A considerable depth of snow has fallen. Three horses died, one belonging to Soteaux,[1] 1 to M. Plant, & 1 to B. Gardipie, unfortunately this loss falls on the individuals who are worst off for horses, and worst able to bear it. The rest of the hunters who started two days ago returned loaded with meat and skins.

Thursdy 3. Overcast some light snow, & blowing fresh most of the day. 4 Beaver were taken.

Friday 4. Mild in the morning, but blew a storm with snow & sleet and drifting afterwards. A party of the people went off to hunt elk. 5 beaver were taken.

---

[1] Soteaux St. Germain. He had been with Ogden in 1824–25. He was with the 1831–32 Snake Country brigade and was lost in the mountains, where he died in July, 1832.

Satdy 5. Thick fog in the morning clear afterwards, cold. The snow is now very hard and crusted which renders it very difficult for the horses to feed.[2]

Sundy 6. Cloudy cold weather, The heat of the sun softens the snow a little in the middle of the day, but it still freezes hard in the night. Three beaver were taken.

Mondy 7. Cloudy stormy weather. Some buffaloe were observed on the opposite side of the river a little way down and some of the people went after them but the ice was so much decayed that they could not venture to cross. 1 Beaver was taken.

Tuesdy 8. Froze keen in the night. Overcast & stormy during the day. The snow wasting very slowly. & the horses becoming leaner daily. Our Indian arrived from the Snake camp, the Snakes have been killing great numbers of buffalo, they run them afoot with snowshoes, the snow is so deep & hard that the poor animals cant escape. Tracks of a small party of Blackfeet have been recently seen in the mountains. On account of the depth of the snow little danger is apprehended from them at present. Two Beaver were taken. Some of the people are making log canoes with which they will be able to hunt in the big river when the ice is entirely gone, more successfully than with horses.

Wedy 9. Froze keen in the night. Blowing fresh and drifting

[2] The following is written in the margin beside this entry:
414
217
24
26
———
681
Work seems to have been making a total of the party's take in furs.

the greater part of the day. One of the men Letendre[3] went to hunt buffalo and brought home a load of meat. The buffaloe are now exceedingly lean and several of them dieing from starvation and the severity of the weather, the depth of the snow and the crust that is upon it renders them unable to run or escape, the weaker ones fall & are unable to get up again. Two beaver were taken.

Thursdy 10. Clear cold weather, the snow thawing a little in the height of the day, but freezing hard again in the night. The horses find much difficulty in feeding. Many of their feet are wounded and bleeding with scraping up the hard crusted snow to get at the grass. Two beaver were taken.

Friday 11. Clear cold stormy weather in the afternoon. 5 beaver were taken, & some traps set.

Saldy 12. Keen frost in the night but the snow wasting a good deal with the heat of the sun during the day. It is only in the afterpart of the day & beginning of the night while the snow is soft that the horses can feed, their feet are cut with the crust in attempting to scrape up the snow in the morning.

Some of the people killed some buffalo, & brought home some meat, it is now very lean. Scarcely eatable.

Sundy 13. Weather the same, every morning the river is runing full of ice, which clears away during the day, and again accumulates in the night. Notwithstanding the quantity of snow on the ground & the coldness of the weather, several summer birds have arrived and the geese, ducks & other waterfowl are passing. The buffalo are also beginning to bring forth their young. the Snake Indians have killed two calves. Five beaver

---

[3] Antoine Le Tendre. He was with the brigade of 1831–32 until his death at the hands of the Blackfeet on October 31, 1831.

& an otter were taken, the ice driving in the large river every morning prevents the beaver going in the traps.

Mondy 14. Raw cold weather, thawed very little during the day, the snow merely softened a little with the heat of the sun, it was towards evening before the river was clear of drift ice. 5 Beaver were taken. Some of the people were in pursuit of buffalo but without success.

Tuesdy 15. Clear cold weather, the snow softens a little in the height of the day but diminished very little. the crust is so hard in the forepart of the day that it bears a person, and the river is driving full of ice every morning. The horses are only able to feed a little in the height & afterpart of the day, the snow is so hard in the morning and after part of the night that they cannot break the crust. 6 Beaver were taken.

Wedy 16. Weather the same. Some of the men were out at the traps three of whom have not returned yet, 3 beaver were taken. The Indians stole a trap and a beaver from Pichette. The Snakes are raising camp and moving down the river. A party of them visited us, and received a little tobacco and some other trifles previous to departing, they will all be off in a few days. They are afraid of the Blackfeet. Some Indians who have been two days up the river hunting, returned & represent the buffalo as dieing in great numbers, they are not able to feed on account of the hardness of the snow.[4]

Thursdy 17. Cloudy cold weather. The Snakes still moving off. The Chief the Horn and a few of the old men paid us a visit previous to departure & remain all night. Some of the men visited their traps, 3 beaver & 1 otter were taken.

[4] The long, severe winter of 1830–31 is generally credited with destroying the buffalo herds of the Snake Country.

Friday 18. Clear cold weather. It was midday before the snow softened any thing worth mentioning. Moved camp to-day across the plain to the little fork of Portneuf's river[5] about 6 or 8 miles, where we have the satisfaction of finding plenty of grass for the horses, in many places clear of snow, though almost every where else the snow lies still a considerable depth. The horses are in much need of such a place, as they are become very lean. I intended to have raised camp two days ago but was deterred by one of the Women F. Payette's Wife who has been ailing some time being so ill that she could not be moved. Four beaver were taken. The Snakes stole two horses in the night one of mine & 1 belonging to C. Plante. We have not yet ascertained what road they were taken. In order to prevent further theft, we commence the night guard this evening, which is not in favour of the horses in their present lean state, but it is better to see them lean than to have them stolen.

Satdy 19. Clear cold weather in the morning. Two more horses were stolen last night one from F Champaigne and one from J Desland. these men turned their horses loose so that they might feed and did not put them in the guard with the others. The above two men and the boy Peerish pursued the thieves and recovered the two horses which were stolen last night and two which were stolen the night before. One of our friends a young Snake was met returning with these two which he had taken from the thieves a good way down the river. He came here with the men & received a reward for his trouble. The thieves took care to be out of the way when the men arrived. Six beaver and two Otters were taken.

Sundy 20. Overcast weather the snow wasting a good deal.

[5] Ross Fork, which is northeast of Pocatello, Idaho. It now flows into the American Falls Reservoir.

The people out in different directions, visiting and setting their traps. 4 beaver were taken.

Monday 21. Blew a storm with snow and sleet all day. Three of the young men who slept out visiting their traps in the Big river returned with three beaver. Notwithstanding the severity of the weather some of the men went to Big river to set their traps farther down but got only a few set, as the river is still frozen over except a small stream in the middle. There are a good many chivereau about our camp. three were killed the day we arrived, & yesterday the boy Peerish killed two.

Tuesdy 22. Stormy with snow and sleet forenoon, fine weather towards evening. Several of the people visited their traps. 7 beaver were taken, 6 in the big river and 1 below, those in the upper part of Portneuf's river caught none. As the small streams were hunted by the Americans in the fall very few are to be found.

Wedy 23. Overcast cold weather. The snow wasting very slowly. The people out in every direction setting their traps. Some went up Portneuf's river to near the mountain where they found it still frozen over.[6] The big river is also barred across with ice in places where there is little current. Two beaver were taken.

Thursdy 24. Stormy with snow and sleet all day.
The severity of the weather did not deter some of the people from visiting the traps. 5 beaver were taken. Several of the men went off yesterday to hunt beaver & have not yet returned.

Friday 25. Cloudy cold weather. Several of the men who had been off two nights at their traps arrived, & those remaining at the camp visited their traps. 20 beaver and 1 Otter were taken.

[6] Near the town of Portneuf, Idaho.

Satdy 26. Stormy with sleet & snow showers. An Indian who has been off two days hunting buffaloe, arrived with some meat very lean. He states numbers of the buffaloe being dead and others on the ground not able to get up and all very lean. None of the people visited their traps.

Sundy 27. Stormy and very cold weather. The snow, notwithstanding the advanced season, wasting very slowly. The people out in different directions visiting their traps. 13 beaver were taken.

Mondy 28. Stormy raw cold weather, sleet & Snow showers.
The people visited their traps. Some went off to sleep some to seek places to set their traps, others to hunt buffalo. 7 beaver were taken.

Tuesdy 29. Weather still cold and stormy became overcast in the evening with a good deal of thunder and some heavy rain. The snow wasted a good deal during the day, indeed this may be reckoned almost the first spring day we have had this season. Several of the men out at their traps, a number of which were taken up Portneuf's river and some small streams are still frozen towards the mountains. Along the shores of the big river and the small channels where the current is not strong, are still frozen. 4 beaver were taken.

Wedy 30. Stormy in the night and all day very cold, froze keen during the night. Two of the men L Pichette & L Rondeau[7] who have been absent down the river three days returned with 10 beaver. Two of the men who were up the big river two

---

[7] Louis Rondeau. He entered the fur trade in 1818 and was with Ogden in 1825–26. Beginning with the season of 1832–33, he served with the Southern party which hunted into California. He retired from company service in 1845.

days returned with their traps having found few or no marks of beaver. F. Payette killed 3 Elk. Some buffalo were seen towards the mountains, but it was too late to go after them. The people are much in want of fresh provisions. Some time past they have been living on their small stock of dry provisions which had been provided for the journey. this I much regret as it will cause a loss of time to replace it, but it could not be avoided, the buffaloe being not only very bad but far off and the horses too lean to go for them.

Thursdy 31. Very cold in the night, and stormy. Stormy & cold during the day, a violent snow storm in the morning.

Some of the men off visiting their traps, but found no beaver. The weather continuing so cold at this late season of the year is greatly against our horses. The new grass is not springing and the old is so dry and withered that there is little or no nourishment in it.

April, 1831

Friday 1. Stormy and very cold with hard frost in the morning towards evening the weather became milder. Some of the men who had traps set above took them up as we mean to move camp tomorrow. There are some beaver where they were set but they are so shy that they cant take them. 5 beaver were taken by some of the men who visited their traps below.

Satdy 2. Clear keen cold weather, the snow scarcely melted any during the day. Moved camp to the junction of Portneuf's river with the Snake river[1] in order to find better feeding for the horses and where we may be able to keep them near the camp. I intended to have moved up the river and hunted about Blackfeet Hill but was for the present deterred from doing so on account of there being little or no grass for the horses in that quarter the buffaloe having eaten it all up, and our horses are still so lean & weak that they absolutely require good feeding for a short time to recruit them a little. Besides the small forks where a chance beaver is likely to be found are still frozen towards the mountain & cant [be] trapped before the ice breaks up. Indeed in the Snake river there is reason to expect but few beaver, scarcely sufficient for the trouble of going for them, did the season admit of our being employed elsewhere to more advantage. In the plain there is still a good deal of snow, ex-

[1] This point is now under water.

cept in spots here & there, where we are encamped has not long been clear of snow. Along the shores of the Snake river there are still bands of ice. Four beaver and an Otter were taken.

Sundy 3. Stormy cold weather. Overcast towards evening. Snow thawing a little. This being Easter the people did not visit their traps.

Mondy 4. Blew a storm and very cold all day, yet a great deal of snow disappeared, little remaining on the low ground, on the higher ground & towards the mountains it appears still to lie a considerable depth. Some of the people revisited their traps, 4 beaver and an otter were taken. Late last night two men, a canadian & a halfbreed, arrived from the American camp on Bear river.[2] Their errand it appears is to buy horses from our people for which purpose they have brought only Beads with them. Very little news has been yet obtained from them regarding their people and what little information they do give seems so exaggerated and improbable that no reliance can be placed upon it. They represent the snow in the mountains as being still of a considerable depth. They came afoot with snowshoes.[3]

Tuesdy 5. Mild weather in the morning, but stormy afterwards. 5 beaver were taken. A number of the people were hunting buffaloe and killed several cows and some calves. The meat though very lean is nevertheless very acceptable, and a seasonable supply to many of the people who have been living on dry meat for a length of time.

[2] Fontanelle's brigade; it wintered on the Bear and Logan Rivers, faring worse than Work's party from the severity of the winter (Ferris, *Life in the Rocky Mountains,* 60–64).

[3] The hard winter and the loss of seventeen head of horses stolen by the Indians had reduced the American party to this extremity (*ibid.,* 63).

Wedy 6. Froze keen in the night. Stormy & bitter cold weather all day. Some of the people visited their traps but no beaver were taken.

Thursdy 7. Clear cold weather. The people visited their traps. 15 beaver were taken. Grass is getting scarce, we prepared to move camp tomorrow.

Friday 8. Light clouds but cold weather.

Moved camp a short distance to across Portneuf's river. One beaver was taken. Several of the people set traps in the Banack river [Bannock Creek] and up Portneuf's river. A Finlay with a party of half breeds expressed a wish to separate from the camp and proceed down the North side of Snake river by Read's river. This I would not permit and it required some trouble to dissuade them from doing so even contrary to my wish. The road they meant to take they were not likely to make any great hunt, and there is every probability they would [have] been pillaged by war parties of Blackfeet and lost all their horses. Besides had they separated from the party we would be too weak to execute the plans we have in view for the summer. These considerations induced me to not allow of their leaving the party. Late in the evening three Flat Heads & a Snake Indian arrived from the American camp which they left two days ago on the opposite side of the mountains, near the head of Portneuf's river.[4] they were making the best of their way to this place which they calculated upon reaching in six days. it is probable they will take much longer time, as their horses and mules are said to be very lean and the snow 3 feet deep for a considerable distance in the mountains. The party consists of 50

[4] Ferris speaks of having descended the South Fork of the Portneuf, which is now named Marsh Creek (*ibid.*, 65).

men headed by Messieurs Fontanelle and Drips, and are on their way to Beaver Head in the Flat Head country.[5]

Satdy 9. Fine mild weather. Did not move camp. The men visited their traps and took 10 beaver which are very few for the number of traps in the water.

Sundy 10. Frost in the night. Fine warm mild weather during the day. Raised camp and marched 12 Miles E. across a point to Portneuf's river near the mountains, in consequence of misinformation, we fell upon the river too high up and find ourselves badly situated for feeding the horses.[6] The grass is barely begining to shoot up, and the old grass of last year is entirely eaten up by the buffaloe. The men who have been a considerable distance up the river with their traps represent the grass as worse the farther up they go. Where the valley is narrow very little ground is clear of snow and some of the small channels still frozen, there are some appearance of beaver. Some buffalo were seen as we passed along. Some of the people went after them, but with little success. Our horses are so very lean & weak that very few of the best runners are able to catch a buffalo that is in any order. 10 beaver were taken.

Mondy 11. Sharp frost in the night, fine weather forenoon but stormy towards evening. Did not move camp today in order to allow the people time to go after buffalo which several of them did but with little success, it is with difficulty our best horses can catch a cow that is in any order. Buffalo are very numerous close too. Several of the men ascended higher up the

---

[5] Andrew Dripps was a noted bourgeois of the American Fur Company. The American party eventually arrived on the Jefferson River in southwestern Montana (*ibid.*, 90).

[6] The camp would be near Batise Springs, Idaho.

river and set traps. 9 beaver were taken, 7 of them brought from the big river by Pichette and Toupin, who slept there last night.

Tuesday 12. Stormy and cold in the morning. Moderate afterwards. Raised camp and proceeded 7 Miles W. N. W. down the river to a better feeding place for our horses. Notwithstanding the advanced season, the grass is barely begining to spring up and the old grass is so dry that there is no nourishment in it so that our horses are getting in order very slowly, and those which the men are hunting with are becoming leaner. 21 beaver were taken today. Sent two men L. Pichette & P. Bernie to visit a little valley called Mr. Ogden's hole where formerly a good many beaver were found & which is not supposed to have been hunted for three years. They found the little river still frozen and a considerable depth of snow along its banks. They found places to set their traps, and suppose there are a few beaver as far as they can judge from the appearance of the river filled up as it is with snow & ice.

Wedy 13. Cloudy cold weather. But few of the people visited their traps, only three beaver were taken. Three men visited Blackfoot river and Snake river above Blackfoot Hill. the ice still remains in the big river except a small channel in the middle. they with difficulty found places to set their traps. The Americans are encamped a little above our last encampment from the opposite side of the Mountains. Some of our Indians visited their camp.

Thursdy 14. Raw cold weather heavy rain in the morning and showry during the day. The people visited their traps. 9 beaver were taken. About noon the Americans arrived and encamped along side of us. the party consists of 57 men headed by Messieurs Fontanelle & Drips gentlemen of respectable appearance,[7] they have been a considerable time crossing the mountains, and met with much difficulty on account of the depth of the snow which occasioned them the loss of several horses. Buffaloe were also scarce and owing to the weakness of their horses difficult to kill, so that they have been for some time short of food. The winter on the opposite side of the winter [*sic*] seems to have been equally severe as we experienced here which is a very unusual thing at Salt Lake. the Snow was very deep a thing, scarcely known formerly. Their intention is to proceed up the Snake river and hunt the left hand fork, (the other two were trapped last summer & fall,) and fall upon some of the head forks of the Missourie, where they expect to meet the Flat Head Indians.[8] They appear to have but very little goods or baggage with them.

Friday 15. Cloudy cold weather. Several of the men visited their traps. 9 beaver were taken. Our people are like to be devoured by the American freemen who seem to be starving, and ready to give anything they have got to procure a little dried meat.

Satdy 16. Snowed the afterpart of the night and nearly all day. it has much more the appearance of a day in January, than one in April. Our American neighbours intended to have moved camp today, but were deterred by the bad weather. Two of our men Bt Tyaquariche and A. Dumais wish to desert from us and accompany the Americans whom they have applied to be received in their employ. Mr. Fontanelle came over and apprised me of the circumstances and stated that he had refused

[7] For the Ferris account of the meeting of the two parties, see *ibid.*, 67.

[8] The left-hand fork of the Snake would be Henry's Fork. The route would take the party to Henry's Lake in southwestern Montana where a barely perceptible divide separates the headwaters of Henry's Fork from the Madison River.

to have any thing to do with them, or to receive some furs which they offered him until they had settled their accounts with me and paid up the debt which they owed the Honbl Hudson's Bay Company. Baptiste declared his determination of accompanying the Iroquois his relations, who deserted from Mr. Ogden some years ago, and who are now with the American party. this Mr. Fontanelle said he could not prevent as they were freemen, but that he could expect no supplies of any kind from him. Were people who have to deal with these scoundrels in this country to act mutually in a similar manner to Mr. Fontanelle there would be much less difficulty with roguish men and they would have less opportunity of putting their knavery in practice. It has been whispered to me that I should not give Bte the horses lent him by the Company, (which I certainly will do,) the Iroquois are determined to take them by force and attempt to play the same game they played with Mr Ogden some years ago.[9] this I have made arrangements to prevent, and am prepared to defeat their purpose even at the expense of the loss of life on both sides.

Sundy 17. Cloudy cold weather, froze keen in the night, the snow as dry in the morning as if it were the middle of the winter, but the heat of the sun melted the most of it during the day.

The Americans took their departure in order to proceed up Snake river. Baptiste came to settle his a/c this morning and paid 15 beaver which is within 4 beaver of the amount of his debts, but he insisted on taking one of the Company's horses which was lent him and giving one which he had left in the hands of the Indians in his place. this I objected to, he never-

[9] The incident occurred on May 20, 1825. A group of Iroquois had been induced to desert by an American party and had attempted to seize the company property from Ogden. For Ogden's report of the matter, see *HBRS*, IV, 296–99.

theless loaded the horse and when I went to take him from him, I observed his Iroquoy friends priming & preparing their arms. I nevertheless seized the horse and though none of them offered to lay a hand on me yet several of them at different times *laid hold of the horse* flogged him till we were all driven into the river, things appearing to become serious F. Payette with the young half breeds of our party, Soteaux St Germain, a Soteaux Indian, & L. Kannota, a Nippising Indian took to their arms to support me. I am sorry I cannot say so of the Canadians of my party either engaged or freemen, P. Bernie, & A. Letendre, both freemen were the only ones that took to their arms, the others looked on with folded arms and left me to struggle for the horse, (which I took back,) without interfering, notwithstanding some of the engaged men were called upon to do so. I would have prevented Baptiste from going off but he gave notice last year not to return to the plains, and being a disabled man from wounds, he would have been an encumbrance at any of the Company's establishments I therefore consider getting clear of him a good riddance. He had two horses of his own which I allowed him to take off.[10] I would have taken one of them for the balance of the debt which he owes but was apprehensive had I done so he would have left his family consisting of a wife & three children on my hands, which would have greatly embarrassed me to take them back to their friends at Walla Walla. I am very glad the affair terminated without bloodshed, it was very near being otherwise, had not Soteaux' *double barrel* gun been seized by someone near him he would have killed one if not two Iroquois and had a shot been fired it is probable few of the Iroquois would have escaped as the half breeds bear an antipathy to them, and when once raised they would not have been easily pacified. Mr. Fontanelle though most of his people moved across the river remained to

[10] Horses were sold to the men by the company but had to be sold back when the men left company service (Merk, *Fur Trade and Empire*, 233).

the last and expressed much regret at the trouble I had with the scoundrel.[11] Dumais when he would not be allowed to go off without paying his debt and returning the Company's horses and traps said nothing more about the matter. Ant. Hoole took up his traps which were set in the big river at Blackfoot Hill, he saw on the opposite side of the river a party of about 50 Blackfeet. these are the first of these Marauders, that have been seen this spring in the plains, though different parties are supposed to be in the mountains. 2 beaver and an otter were taken.

Monday 18. Frost in the night. Cloudy mild weather. Did not raise camp in order to allow the men to take up all their traps which were in the water. 9 beaver were taken.

Tuesdy 19. Overcast but rather mild weather. Raised camp and proceeded 10 Miles S. to the Banack river, (a small stream,) near the mountains.[12] Our intention is to ascend this little river and hunt its heads and the heads of two other little rivers which the Indians report to be rich in beaver and to have never yet been hunted by the Whites. From the quantity of snow on the mountains we are apprehensive that the upper part of the river remains still frozen over and that the valley through which it runs is not yet clear of snow

It was our original plan to have ascended the Snake river to the forks and have hunted about that neighbourhood, previous to crossing the mountains to the Southward, but we have been induced to abandon the idea of doing so, from ascertaining that the Americans trapped that track of country last fall. the few beaver we would be likely to obtain would not be adequate to the loss of time, as this late season, which, may be much more

[11] Ferris states that Soteaux pointed his gun at Fontanelle. As Work was completely occupied with the horse, his account must be based on the statements of others (Ferris, *Life in the Rocky Mountains*, 67).

[12] The camp would be on Bannock Creek near the Indian school.

advantageously employed elsewhere. Our trapping operations would be likely to be very soon stopped by the spring floods. It is also to be apprehended that we would be too short of ammunition to contend with the numerous parties of hostile Blackfeet we would be soon to meet with, the small quantity I have remaining would be far from adequate, and the men have so squandered their years supply which they received at Vancouver that but very few have any remaining, the most of them having received supplies from me for some time back. The Americans are going that road and by trapping as well as would render the chance of getting any thing worth while for our trouble still less. A party of Blackfeet, passed close by our camp last night or early this morning, their tracks led to the mountains, the party is supposed to consist of 15 or 20 men. One of the men saw a person running buffaloe yesterday which he supposed to be a Blackfoot Indian. Some of the men who ascended the Banack river with their traps found an encampment which had been occupied by Blackfeet only 2 or 3 days ago. they are supposed to be the same party which were reconnoitering our camp last night. They have a few horses which they are supposed to have stolen, with which they probably wished to make their way to their own country but were probably afraid to venture out in the plains lest they would be stopped by some of our party. Several of the people ran some buffalo a few of which were killed but they are so lean that they are scarcely fit to eat.

Wedy 20. Cold stormy weather. Did not raise camp in order to allow the people to kill buffalo, (large herds of which were close to,) and dry some provisions to replace what they have consumed, but I regret that very few were killed and those very lean. Indeed our horses are still so lean and weak that very few of them are able to catch a buffalo particularly if it happens to be in a little order. Four beaver were taken.[13]

Thursdy 21. Stormy raw cold weather. Moved camp and marched 10 Miles S. E. up the river. The river here is a narrow deep stream with steep clayey banks which have some willows growing upon them, and appears well adapted for beaver. A good many marks of which are to be seen. This little stream is not known to have ever been hunted by whites. Just above our last encampment it spreads out into a kind of swamp which was probably taken by the hunters to be its source. The valley through which the river runs here is pretty wide and seems to have been but a very short time free of snow. the mountains on each side of it remain in sundry places along the shores of the river. The valley seems to produce little else but wormwood, there is a little coarse dry grass on some points along the river. Owing to the unusual lateness of the spring, the young grass is barely begining to shoot up so that our horses lean as they are can gather very little to eat which is much against them and retards our progress, as it is out of power to make such days journies as we could wish. Some of the people went in pursuit of buffaloe but with little success. Nearly all the people set their traps. Only 2 beaver were taken. Two of the men A. Finlay and A. Hoole who went after buffaloe towards the mountains discovered a party of 14 Blackfeet with 8 or 10 horses, the Indians immediately fled and the men foolishly pursued them some distance before they returned to the camp. On their arrival a party immediately went in pursuit of them, but could not overtake them, they had got across the mountain notwithstanding the depth of the snow. F. Payette and 4 or 5 of the half breeds ascended the mountain after them, but it was too late to continue the pursuit and they returned. A mare &

---

[13] This entry finishes the first of the notebooks John Work used for this journal. Subsequent entries are on loose sheets which were pierced for thongs used in binding them within leather covers. This portion of the journal was titled "Part Two" by Work, an arrangement he retained in the fair copy made for the governor and committee in London.

colt which they left in their hurry was brought to the camp. There were the tracks of some women and children with the party. It is conjectured that the horses were stolen from the Snakes and that the women and children are also of that nation and made slaves of by the Blackfeet.[14] They threw away several cords in their haste. A. Letendre who was up the river setting his traps saw three Blackfeet with a horse, they immediately went of[f]. P. Bernie & L. Kanotta saw & pursued another party of 5 men, two of them in their haste to escape threw away their robes and cords. It is to be regretted that the two men who saw the party with the horses did not come to apprise us at the camp immediately and the whole party with their horses would probably have been taken.

Friday 22. Cloudy cold weather, some heavy rain and sleet in the night and the forepart of the day. Did not move camp. The people visited their traps and set some more. 25 beaver and 1 Otter were taken. There is the appearance of a good many beaver.

Satdy 23. Stormy cold weather. Moved camp 5 miles farther up the river in order to find some feeding for the horses, and even here the grass is very indifferent and scarcely any of it, though there are few buffaloe to be seen now, they have been very numerous here short ago and eat up most of what little grass was. The men visited their traps and took 33 beaver. The river here divides into to [*sic*] forks one falls in from the Eastward the other runs from the South,[15] the former is that which the Indians represented to be richest in beaver. We are mortified to find that as far as the men proceeded up it, it is choked up with snow except in small spots here and there, and the val-

---

[14] Such captures by the Blackfeet were not uncommon. The most notable example of this was the famous Sacajawea.

[15] Rattlesnake Creek is the east fork; the south fork is Bannock Creek.

ley through which it runs, *though of considerable extent*, still covered with snow to a considerable depth in places 3 to 4 feet deep, and farther up probably much deeper. The men who went farthest up the S. branch 15 or 20 Miles suppose they have reached its head a kind of swamp here though the valley is larger than in the other branch yet the snow lies equally deep, and farther on through a fine valley appears still deeper. *the wormwood is covered with the snow.* In this state of the snow we can neither trap these little rivers in the mountains at present, nor attempt to cross the mountains without the risk of losing several of our horses from the depth of the snow and want of food. the only step we can take now is to abandon this road and seek another pass more practicable. it would take too much time to wait till the snow melts. Thus are the prospects of the little hunt which we expected to make of 600 or 700 beaver in this quarter blasted. The unprecedented lateness of the spring is greatly against our operations. the oldest hands even in the severest winters never witnessed the season so late. The men saw some buffaloe on the verge of the snow, probably they have been driven there by the Blackfeet Indians whom we found here. the people killed some of the buffalo but they were so lean that they were scarcely eatable. Three of the men drove a herd of bulls into a bank of snow yesterday and killed 16 of them.

Sundy 24. Frost in the morning. Clear cold weather, for the season, during the day. The men visited their traps, 14 beaver were taken. the water is rising which is against the trappers. Two of the men saw 6 Blackfeet Indians high up the river yesterday, they made to the mountains. Some were prowling about our camp last night, the tracks of two who passed close to in the night were observed this morning.

Mondy 25. Cloudy cold weather. Returned down the river

to near our encampment of the 20th. The people visited their traps but only one beaver was taken. The water in the little river rose several feet in the night. Though only a days journey from our encampment of this morning, there is a material change in the appearance of the country. Vegetation has here made considerable progress, and we found pretty good feeding for our horses.

Tuesdy 26. Rained the greater part of the day, light in the morning but heavy towards evening. Moved camp and marched 10 Miles S. W. across a point to Snake river.[16] Here we have the satisfaction to find excellent feeding for the horses. One beaver was taken in the morning. The men were out in different directions setting their traps. Some buffalo were seen and two or three of them killed in the plains, they are still very lean. The hunters observed the fresh tracks of some parties of Blackfeet, and thought they saw one on horseback. One of the parties have a few horses with them which they have probably stolen from the Snakes.

Wedy 27. Heavy rain in the night and stormy with rain all day. The unfavourable weather deterred us from raising camp. The people visited their traps, and set some more, 20 beaver were taken, 16 of them in a small rivulet towards the foot of the mountains which appears never to have been trapped nor even known, notwithstanding parties of trappers having so frequently passed this road. C. Plant, M. Plant, Bt. Dubrille[17] & J. Desland found it yesterday.

Thursdy 28. Cloudy fair weather. Moved camp and proceeded 6 Miles down Snake river to near American falls. Here

[16] The camp site would be near Rainbow Beach.
[17] Baptiste Dubruille. He had served Astor's Pacific Fur Company and the Northwest Company in the Pacific Northwest. He retired to settle in the Willamette Valley.

we have good feeding for the horses. All hands out visiting and setting their traps. 23 beaver and 2 Otters were taken, 11 of the beaver from the little creek in the plains. Below the rapids there is some appearance of beaver, notwithstanding the Americans passed this way last fall. Some of our hunters had trapped the big river down to near the falls early in the spring.

Friday 29. Stormy weather, very heavy rain mixed with hail and sleet. The unfavorable weather deterred us from moving camp, but it did not prevent the people from visiting their traps and setting several more. 19 beaver were taken.

Satdy 30. Heavy overcast weather with some rain in the morning. Cloudy fine weather afternoon.

The unfavourable appearance of the weather in the morning prevented us from raising camp. The men visited their traps and took near 50 beaver in a small creek called the big stone river.[18] This little stream appears to have been hunted by the Americans last fall, yet there are marks of beaver being still pretty numerous.

Several of the peoples horses became jaded and gave up by the way, some had to be left behind, and it was dark by the time others reached the encampment. The poor horses are still so lean and weak that they are unable to bear any kind of a hard days work. they are much in want of a week's repose and good feeding but the lateness of the season, will not admit of our allowing them so much.

[18] Rock Creek. Work also calls it Rock River. It enters the Snake on the south midway between the mouths of Bannock Creek and Raft River. The stream Work refers to on May 27 as Big Stone River is Salmon Falls Creek.

May, 1831

Sundy 1. Heavy cloudy weather, some Showers in the afternoon. Moved camp and proceeded 12 Miles S. by W. across a point to the little creek where the people have their traps set near the mountains,[1] the road though a little hilly was good, considerable patches of snow still occupy the north sides of the little hills and the bottoms of the deep gullies.

This little river is a narrow deep stream, resembling the river Banack, running between steep clayey banks. Where we are encamped is at the entrance of the mountains, the valley is not wide and no wood but some willows on the banks of the river. There is pretty good feeding for the horses, but farther up the valley where the snow has but very lately disappeared, the men represent the grass as very indifferent, in many places scarcely any. All hands visited their traps 65 beaver & 1 Otter were brought to the camp, but the greater part of these were taken yesterday and left in cache, the traps this morning did not yield according to expectation.

Mondy 2. Cloudy fine weather. Did not move camp in order to allow the horses to feed pretty good grass being at this place, and to allow the men time to take up their traps before we descend again to the Snake river. Some of the people have

[1] Rock Creek. The camp would be near the present community of Rockland, Idaho.

been up this river as far as there is any wood or beaver. 11 Beaver were taken. Some of the men have set their traps in the big river.

Tuesdy 3. Cloudy, fine warm weather afternoon. Stormy with thunder and some rain towards evening. Moved camp and proceeded 10 Miles S. W. to the Snake river where we encamped among hills on the Small Crawfish river. The road very hilly and fatiguing on the horses many of whom were much fatigued on reaching the encampment. They are recompensed by excellent grazing. The men were on a head setting their traps. 12 beaver & 1 Otter were taken.

Wedy 4. Cloudy stormy weather. Marched 10 Miles W. S. W. to Raft river which fell upon 10 or 15 Miles from its junction with Snake river,[2] the road good, but very hilly the forepart of the journey. Raft river is now very high and muddy, owing to the melting of the snow. There are some appearance of beaver in it though this part of it was hunted by the Americans last fall. The men visited and changed their traps. 11 beaver were taken. Some herds of buffalo were seen on the opposite side of Snake river, and the tracks of some herds ascending this river. We have it possible to procure a stock of provisions as we have a long way to march through a country nearly destitute of Animals of any kind, and this is the last place where we are likely to find any buffaloe.

Thursdy 5. Cloudy stormy weather, thunder and some very heavy rain towards evening.

Marched about five miles south up the river where we en-

---

[2] The detailed footnotes, beginning with this one and continuing through May 23, are by Professor David E. Miller. The field research was financed by grants from the University of Utah.

This camp was on the east side of Raft River, probably near the junction of Hegler Creek and the Raft.

camped,[3] and sent most of the people after a large herd of buffalo which was discovered feeding in the mountain. Several were killed. Our horses have improved a little and are now able to catch them. The buffaloe are begining to get in a little better order, and though scarcely the appearance of fat is to be found on them the meat is tolerably palatable. The people visited their traps in the morning. 14 beaver were taken. Gave orders for the people not to go ahead lest they would disturb the buffaloe and drive them farther off.

Friday 6. Cloudy fine weather. Did not move camp in order to allow the people to dry the meat which was killed yesterday. The buffaloe are so lean now that three scarcely yields as much dry meat, and of an inferior quality, as one would do in the fall or early part of the winter. 5 Beaver were taken.

Satdy 7. Cloudy fine weather. Marched 12 Miles South up the river.[4] The road good, but very indifferent feeding for the horses. A number of the people went after a herd of buffalo which was grazing on the opposite side of the river and killed several, the meat of which the women are now busy drying. It is fortunate we find buffaloe here as it saves us the trouble of going a long day's march out into the plains to the Eastward to a place called the Fountain where buffaloe are always said to be found.[5] It would at least lose three days going to this place. I had some trouble in preventing some of the men from running ahead of the camp with their traps and raising the

[3] After crossing Hegler Creek the expedition proceeded five miles southward along the east bank of the river. Buffalo were evidently sighted in the hills to the east.

[4] Still on the east side of Raft River, the expedition camped almost directly east of Malta, Idaho. Buffalo were hunted this day on the west side of Raft River, in the vicinity of Malta.

[5] The "Fountain" probably refers to the Lava Springs area on Portneuf River where earlier Hudson's Bay Company expeditions had found plenty of buffalo.

Animals. Some of them want no provisions themselves and are indifferent whether the others have it in their power to get any or not. By missing the opportunity of collecting a little provisions now the people would be obliged to eat several of their horses before reaching the fort, as animals of any kind are very scarce. — Beaver were taken.[6]

Sundy 8. Cloudy fine weather. Marched 12 Miles South up the river.[7] The road still good, but grass for the horses very indifferent. A number of the people went in pursuit of a large herd of buffaloe which was feeding on the opposite side of the river, and killed a number of them, the meat of which is now being dried. Blackfeet are still following our camp. Two of the young men who went out in the plain yesterday to discover buffaloe saw three but were not sure on account of the haze whether it was men or Antelopes. Two of the men who went back this morning for some traps which they had behind saw three Indians coming to our camp after all the people had left it some time. — Beaver were taken.

Mondy 9. Fine weather. Did not raise camp in order to allow the people time to kill some more buffaloe. Some large herds were found along the foot of the mountains on this side of the river. A number of whom were killed.[8] The most of the people have now nearly enough of provisions. What little a few of the people still want we expect to find as we advance up the river. Some marks of Blackfeet were seen near the camp this morning. In the morning the buffaloe were observed flying from the

---

[6] In this entry and the following one there is a blank in the manuscript. Either no beaver were taken or Work forgot to enter the number.

[7] Camp was located near present-day Bridge, Idaho, on the east side of the Raft River. The buffalo were killed on the west side.

[8] These buffalo were probably feeding on the north slopes of the Raft River Mountains from which point they fled eastward, doubtless through Kelton Pass via Strevell, Idaho.

mountains to the Eastward, and it is conjectured they were disturbed by a band of those maurauders.

Tuesdy 10. Unpleasant stormy weather. Raised camp and proceeded 10 Miles South up the river the Roche where it becomes confined in a narrow valley.[9] here we find good feeding for the horses. No buffaloe to be seen today until towards evening when a small band were observed in the mountain. Some of the people went after them, but only one was killed. One of the men M. Plante who went after the buffaloe was behind the other men when returning and discovered a Blackfoot Indian on horseback and fired upon him but missed the Indian made off towards the mountain, where five other Blackfeet were observed afoot. These scamps are still following us seeking an opportunity to steal.

Wedy 11. Cloudy cold weather. Marched 10 Miles S. S. W. up the river, the road good. We deviated a little from our straight road today in order to send off a party of our men to hunt in another direction tomorrow. The people visited some traps which were set yesterday & took 6 beaver. No buffaloe, nor the marks of any to be seen today.[10]

Thursdy 12. Fine weather in the morning, but heavy rain and snow and very cold afterwards. Raised camp and marched

[9] Although the journal indicates a southern direction, this day's route veered to the southwest, still following the main fork of the Raft River. Some ten miles southwest of Bridge the river cuts through a narrow, rocky gorge. Just west of the narrows the camp was pitched. The buffalo sighted this day were doubtless on the south side of the valley where Yost, Utah, is located today.

[10] A short distance west of the camp of May 10 the expedition reached the main forks of Raft River, Edwards Fork coming in from the northwest and the main branch coming from the south-southwest. Work's party followed the main branch for ten miles and camped approximately two miles south of the Utah-Idaho line and five miles west of Yost.

10 miles S. across the mountains and encamped on a small rivulet of snow water, the head of Raft river appears in a deep valley to the West of us.[11] The road over the mountains hilly and rugged and some places very boggy. The snow still lies in banks of considerable depth, and appears to have but very recently disappeared off the most of the ground. The grass is barely begining to spring up except on small spots exposed to the South which has been some time clear of snow where vegetation has made some progress. From the ruggedness of the road and the badness of the weather this was a harrassing day both on horses and people for want of water we could not encamp sooner.

In order that we make a better hunt I separated our party this morning and sent 8 men viz. C. Plante (who is in charge of the party,) J. Desland, F. Champaigne, L. Rondeau, L. Quintall, A. Dumais, Bt. Dubrielle and A. Longtain to hunt to the Westward on the heads of the small rivers which fall into Snake river and on the Eastern fork of Sandwich Island river,[12] while I with the remainder of the party proceed to the Southward to Ogden's river[13] and then to the heads of Sandwich Island river. Plante was directed to push on and make a good

11 At this point Raft River runs through a narrow, winding canyon from Junction Valley eastward through the mountain. Rather than thread this canyon Work chose to leave the stream and turn to the south. The route took him over a low divide to the southwest into Junction Valley and thence southward, keeping rather high along the slopes of its eastern side. In clear view below him to the west was the Raft River, which heads in the mountains to the south and, at this point, runs northward through a deep valley. Lynn, Utah, is located on its west bank. After a very difficult, rough journey of ten miles the party camped on a small tributary some three miles southwest of Lynn.

12 Owyhee River. The east fork is now known as Blue Creek.

13 Humboldt River. Ogden had called it Unknown River when he still had hopes that it might be the Bonaventura, a river that early mapmakers invented to connect the Salt Lake basin with San Francisco Bay. The trappers called it Paul's River, after Joseph Paul who died and was buried near the Carson Sinks in Nevada.

encampment today so that he might get out of the reach of the Blackfeet who are still following our track but instead of doing so, some of the people who went in pursuit of a horse that followed the party found them encamped only a few miles from our last night's station. If they push on they will in a short time be out of reach of the Blackfeet.

Friday 13. Raw cold weather froze keen in the night.

Marched about 15 miles S. E. to the entrance of the plain of great Salt Lake.[14] The road very hilly and rugged, numerous gullies to pass several of whom are still full of snow through which the horses sometimes with difficulty dragged themselves. Nearly all this days journey through the mountains the snow has but very recently disappeared, even in patches, and the ground is still so imbibed with water that the horses nearly bog in it except in a few spots here and there the grass is barely begining to shoot up and in many places vegetation is not yet commenced. Where we are encamped there is a little grass for the horses. This was a fatiguing day on both men and horses. Many of the latter with difficulty reached the encampment.

Satdy 14. Cloudy cold weather. Marched 12 Miles S. along the foot of the mountains and encamped on a small river on Mr. Ogden's usual road to Ogden's river. The road today was good and pretty level though intersected by several gullies some of which are still full of snow. The Mountains to the W. are still partially covered with snow and appear very rugged, to the Eastward lies the great plain thickly studded with clumps

[14] This day's march took the expedition over the rim of the Great Basin to the headwaters of Dove Creek, which stream was followed southeastward out of the mountains and onto the plain of Great Salt Lake. The main road between Park Valley and Lynn follows virtually the same route today. This night's camp was located on Dove Creek, probably a short distance above the point where Utah Highway 70 crosses that stream, a half-dozen miles southwest of Rosette, Utah.

of hills.[15] About this neighborhood we expected to find some buffaloe and that such of the people as are short of provisions would furnish themselves with some more, but not a mark of a buffaloe is to be seen. There are a good many antelopes in the plains and some black tail chivereau.

Sundy 15. Cloudy fine weather, the air rather cool in the neighborhood of the Snow clad Mountains.

Proceeded on our journey 8 Miles South where we encamped on a small rivulet which barely yields sufficient water for the horses.[16] No water being to be found near was the cause of us putting up so early at this place. The road lay along the foot of the mountains and though hilly was good. it was intersected by several gullies some of which are still full of snow, larger hills and points of mountains lay below us and the plains than yesterday.

Found an Old Snake Indian woman she said her people were encamped near some of the people. also found three men of the same nation with horses, these people seldom venture from the mountains, they are now employed collecting roots, one of them have yet ventured to our camp.

Mondy 16. Cloudy cool weather in the morning, fine weather afterwards. Continued our route 13 Miles S to what is called the fountain, which is a small spring of indifferent brackish

---

[15] Keeping west of present Highway 70, the route this day led somewhat west of south to the spring at present Rosebud Ranch. This beautiful spring of fresh water was to become a major stopping place for future travelers through the area. In clear view to the west was the Muddy Range with several peaks well over seven thousand feet in elevation, still covered with snow. Work's description of the area is excellent. The expedition struck Peter Skene Ogden's route on May 13 at Dove Creek and followed it most of the way to the Humboldt.

[16] Continuing southward among the foothills, the brigade found water at a small, unnamed stream near the east end of the Bovine Range.

water in the plain where the soil is mixed with saline matter.[17] Not only water is scarce here but there is very little grass for our horses. The road though hilly was pretty good. It lay down a deep gully and over several hills before we reached the plain, ranges of mountains covered with snow run along to the Westward, besides the plain is studded with detached hills several of whom are still covered with snow. On reaching the plain it appears to the Eastward like an immense lake with *black* rocky hills here and there like islands. large tracts of the plain appears perfectly white and destitute of any kind of vegetables, it is said to be composed of white clay. A small lake appears in it at some distance. To the South East is the Uta lake and river,[18] to the Southward the country is said to be destitute of water for a long way, yet snow topped mountains appear in that direction. We found a few Snake Indians encamped here and a party of 20 men visited us from farther out in the plain.[19] Some leather and other trifles were traded from them by the people.

Tuesday 17. Fine weather. Continued our March 11 Miles W. S. W. to a small rivulet of indifferent brackish water which

[17] The party evidently skirted the east end of the Bovine Range rather than going through Immigrant Pass, since the journal makes no reference to such a pass but constantly mentions the snow-covered mountains lying to the west.

The "fountain" here described is a small spring located directly south of the east end of the Bovine and slightly northeast of Pigeon Mountain. Today it is very much as it was when Work described it in 1831. A few wild roses have sprung up around it; scrubby sage covers the whole area. The small stream is soon lost in the desert. In the early spring temporary lakes cover the low ground.

[18] Far off to the southeast Work could see the snow-capped peaks of the Stansbury, Oquirrh, and Wasatch mountains. His mention of "Uta lake and river" does not mean that he could see them. He knew merely that they were there, having learned of them from the trappers in his party.

[19] There are numerous small, brackish springs in the desert southeast of the "fountain." The visiting Indians had doubtless come from these water holes.

winds through a salt marshy valley.[20] There is pretty good feeding for the horses. The road pretty good and level, though
there are detached hills on every side of us. The rivulet is lost
in the plain a little below our encampment.

Wedy 18. Fine warm weather. Proceeded 7 Miles W. S. W.
up the little rivulet which continues of the same appearance and
about the same size. We encamped early on account of no water
being found farther on, tomorrow we have a very long encampment to make.[21]

Thursdy 19. Cloudy fine warm weather. Continued our journey at an early hour and Marched 25 Miles S. S. W. to a range
of Mountains which we crossed and thence across a plain to a
small rivulet which we found unexpectedly in the middle of
it.[22] The road good but hilly crossing the mountains. Not a
drop of water to be found all the way. We luckily found water
near 2 hours march sooner than we expected, yet several of the

[20] A march of eleven easy miles brought the company to Grouse Creek
near the present site of Lucin. Camp was established a short distance upstream,
west and north of Lucin.

[21] Three miles northwest of Lucin, Grouse Creek, which comes in from
the north, is joined by Thousand Springs Creek from the west. The latter
stream drains the whole Thousand Springs Valley and may very well have
been larger than the north branch (Grouse Creek) when Work arrived. At
least he seems to have considered it the main branch. Thousand Springs Creek
flows almost straight south for six miles before entering Montello Valley,
then makes a sharp bend to the northeast to join Grouse Creek some ten
miles distant. The Work party doubtless followed this stream from the con-
fluence southwestward and camped a couple of miles east of the big bend.
There is a stock reservoir at the site today.

[22] This long day's march took the brigade southwestward through Montello Valley, over the easy pass now used by the Southern Pacific Railroad,
and into the north end of Goshute Valley, where water was unexpectedly
found, probably on the east branch of Squaw Creek. The day's actual destination seems to have been the big springs at Johnson Ranch, seven miles
southwest of Oasis. The unexpected water allowed the party to camp two
hours short of its destination.

horses were much jaded some of them nearly giving up. That and the dirt were more oppressive upon them than the distance they came. The mountains round this valley or plain are not very high, yet in places still covered with snow. The tracks of elk, black tail deer, & sheep were seen in the Mountains but could not be approached. Cabrie[23] are seen in the plains, but all very shy. The hunters saw some Indians, the naked wretches fled to the mountains. None of them visited our camp.

Friday 20. Fine warm weather. Continued our course 12 Miles S. S. W. across the plain where we encamped on a small stream of brackish water which runs through a salt marsh and in a short distance is lost in the plain.[24]

Satdy 21. Fine weather, *A thunder storm and a little rain.* Proceeded on our journey 16 Miles W. S. W. over a rugged stony though not high mountain and thence across a plain to a lake where we have the satisfaction to find good water. The road over the Mountains stony and rugged, but across the plain very good. A range of high Mountains covered with snow appears ahead of us.[25]

Some Antelopes are seen in the Plains but no appearance of any other Animals.

Sunday 22. Sultry warm weather. Marched 20 Miles W. N. W. to the W end of a steep snowy Mountain where we

[23] The prong-horned antelope.

[24] Continuing southward through Goshute Valley, the expedition found water in a small stream now labeled "Hardy Creek" on some maps. Camp was pitched at a point slightly north and some four miles west of Shafter. There is an abandoned ranch house there today.

[25] This day the party crossed the Pequop Range by way of Shafter Pass, traversed Independence Valley, and camped at the east end of Snow Water Lake, which probably extended several miles farther east than it does now. The snow-capped Ruby Mountains lay directly in front of them.

encamped on a small creek which issues from the mountain, the waters of which are lost in the plain below.[26] This morning we left Mr. Ogden's track to Ogden's river in hopes to reach the river sooner and fall upon it a few days march higher up than by the usual route. Our road good, lay through an extensive plain. From the heat of the day and the distance marched, the horses were much jaded and the people fatigued on reaching the encampment. However we have good water and excellent feeding for the horses.

Seven naked starved looking Indians visited the camp. We have been seeing the tracks of these people every day, but seldom any of them venture to approach us.

Monday 23. Warm weather. Continued our journey at an early hour and marched 16 miles W. N. W. through a small difile and across the end of the mountain and down a plain to the E. fork of Ogden's river. This branch runs through a low part of the plain which is now a swamp owing to the height of the water, the river having overflowed its banks.[27] Several of

[26] Leaving the east end of Snow Water Lake, the brigade now turned to the north-northwest and, after traveling twenty miles, camped in the north-west corner of Clover Valley at the southwest base of a spur of the East Humboldt Range.

This day Work left Ogden's track of 1828–29 in order to strike the Humboldt above the point where Ogden had left it three years earlier. This is an important clue to the Work route and definitely places his track much farther south than has formerly been believed. Ogden states that he left the Humboldt December 18, 1828, and traveled east "over a large range of high hills and descended a very high hill where we reached a fine level plain with scarcely any snow. Here we found a small lake and encamped at dusk." (T. C. Elliott, ed., "Journal of Peter Skene Ogden; Snake Expedition, 1828– 29," *OHQ*, XI [1910] 388ff.) Ogden left the Humboldt River a short distance west of present Halleck, traveled east through Secret Pass into Secret Valley, climbed the south end of the East Humboldt Range, and descended to the west side of Snow Water Lake. He returned over the same route in April, 1829, crossed the river and traveled downstream some distance.

[27] A narrow defile cuts off the easternmost extension of the East Humboldt Range but offers easy access from the north end of Clover Valley to

the people were ahead both up and down the river with their traps. No vestiges of beavers are to be seen on the fork where we are encamped though some of the people ascended it to near the mountains. In the middle or principal fork the water is so high that the river can only be approached in places the banks being overflowed, and the low ground in its neighbourhood inundated. It is difficult to discover any marks of beaver. Nevertheless several traps were set at a venture.

Tuesdy 24. Warm sultry weather. Marched 15 Miles W. N. W. across the plain to the middle fork of the river.[28] We had some difficulty crossing the E. fork several of the horses bogged in its swampy banks. The road across the plain pretty good, the low ground through which the river runs is nearly all flooded. The river here has a good deal of willows on its banks. Only three beaver were taken. The people begin to apprehend there are but few beaver in the river, and from the height of the water, those few cannot be taken. This part of the river was hunted two years ago by a party of hunters which Mr. Ogden sent this way. They found a good many beaver and supposed the river was not clean trapped.

Wedy 25. Overcast, Thunder and heavy rain afternoon.

Proceeded 10 Miles up the river which here runs from N. to S. the road good.[29] The banks of the river everywhere overflowed. Four beaver and 1 Otter were taken. The part of the river we passed today is well wooded with willows and appears admirably adapted for beaver yet few appear to be in it. A party

---

the Humboldt River. Work evidently followed this route, arriving at the East Fork about midway between Wells and Deeth, Nevada.

[28] Marys River. The party is about fifteen miles northeast of Deeth, Nevada.

[29] The valley is level and fairly wide at this point. The camp would be in the area which is currently cropped in hay. The Indians were probably Paiutes, as this would be within their territorial limits.

of Indians visited our camp this morning and exchanged two horses with the people. Some of the people were out hunting. F. Payette & L. Kanotte killed each an Antelope, these are the only Animals to be seen here, and they are so shy that it is difficult to kill any of them. Several of the people are getting short of provisions, and not finding beaver here as was expected is discouraging the people.

Thursdy 26. Overcast weather blowing fresh. Did not raise camp in order to allow our horses to feed and repose a little, of which they are in much want, they have been marching 16 days without one days rest, they are all very lean and many of them much jaded. I was still expecting to find some beaver that we might allow the horses to recruit a little and hunt at the same time and was induced to push on even to the injury of some of the horses.

The people visited their traps but only four beaver were taken. Those who went farthest up the river bring no better accounts of the appearance of beaver. The water is falling a little above. A party of Snakes Indians visited us, they inform us that there are some small streams in the mountains where there are a few beaver.

Fridy 27. Cloudy fine weather. Continued our journey 12 Miles North up the river to a small branch which falls in from the North, the Main stream runing here from the West. The head of this small fork is close to the head of the Big stone river[30] which falls into Snake river. The road pretty good till we reached the fork where on account of the water it is a perfect bog and we had much difficulty in crossing it, several of the

---

[30] The stream that Work refers to on April 30 above as the Big Stone River is Rock Creek. It heads far to the north and east of here. This is obviously a mistake, and the stream should be Salmon Falls Creek, which does head in this general vicinity.

horses bogged and some of the things were wet. 4 beaver were taken. No better signs of beaver. Some of the people were hunting Antelopes, which are the only animals to be seen here, but only one was killed.

Satdy 28. Stormy cold weather. Proceeded on our journey 10 Miles W up the river to above where it is enclosed between steep rocky hills.[31] the road part of the way very hilly and rugged and so stony that the horses ran much risk of breaking their legs. Here we found a place where the river is fordable, the water has subsided a little within these few days. During this days march the river is well wooded with poplar & willows yet there is very little appearance of beaver. Only 3 were taken today. Four of the young men who left camp on the 25th arrived in the evening. they struck across the country to the W. fork of the river which they ascended to the Mountains and did not find a mark of a beaver to induce them to put a trap in the water. That branch like the one we are on has overflowed its banks. The young men on the way here passed two small streams which run towards Snake river.[32]

Sundy 29. Stormy raw cold weather. Crossed the river in the morning and proceeded across the Mountains 10 Miles S. S. W. to a small stream which falls into Bruneau's river.[33]

[31] The river here has carved a narrow channel through a lava flow. The country is extremely rocky with chunks of rock broken off the flow and the lava itself has very little overburden. The camp would be about fifteen miles southeast of Charleston, Nevada.

[32] The fork of the river mentioned is now known as the North Fork of the Humboldt River. The men may have crossed two small streams at the head of Bruneau River or, by going a few miles northwest before turning east, the head of Bruneau River and the South Fork of the Owyhee River.

[33] Passing some ten miles south of Charleston, Nevada, the party arrived on the Bruneau River south of the junction of the North Fork and Charleston roads. The river has been dammed and the swamp is now a water tank in the early summer and good pasture in the late summer.

The road hilly and rugged and very swampy on the banks of the little river which we crossed. There is still a good deal of snow in large banks in the mountains. it appears not to have been long since disappeared in the valleys as the grass is still very short and vegetation but little advanced. A few of the people who imagined the river was not fordable above remained at a narrow part in the rocks yesterday evening and made a bridge by felling trees so that they fell across the river over which they carried their baggage, but in crossing their horses one belonging to G. R. Rocque was drowned.

Mondy 30. Mild weather in the morning which was succeeded by a violent thunder storm with hail and snow which continued a considerable time. Stormy cold weather during the remainder of the day. The unfavourable weather deterred us from raising camp.

Thursdy 31.[34] Stormy cold weather, some showers in the morning, & a heavy snow storm in the evening. Keen frost last night. Continued our journey 13 Miles across the Mountains to a small stream which we suppose falls into Sandwich Island river.[35] The road very hilly and rugged being over a number of deep gullies, there is also a good deal of snow in the Mountains, some bars of which we had to cross. The country has a bare appearance. Not an animal except a chance antelope to be seen.

[34] This error in the day continues throughout the remainder of the journal.

[35] The route here is roughly parallel to the road from State Highway 43 to Charleston. The stream is, in most years, a dry wash, but the exceptionally high water in the spring of 1831 accounts for this and a number of other "streams" encountered by Work in northern Nevada and southeastern Oregon.

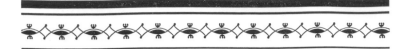

June, 1831

Fridy 1. Keen frost in the night. Stormy cold weather during the day. Continued our route 12 Miles W. across the mountains and down into the valley where a number of small branches fall in from the mountains and form the head of the E fork of Sandwich island river.[1] This little valley is about 20 miles long & 15 wide. a small fork falls in from the S, 2 from the E, and 1 from the W. all of which form one stream which runs to the N. W. through a narrow channel bounded by impassable rocks. The different forks in the valley have some willows on their banks and seem well adapted for beaver, yet the men who have been out in every direction setting their traps complain that the marks of beaver are scarce. The water has been lately very high and all[2] the plain overflowed but it is now subsiding. To the Southward there is a small height of land which separates the waters of this river from a fork of Ogden's river [North Fork of the Humboldt], to the Westward there is a high rugged Mountain covered with Snow. Our road today was very rugged & hilly & in many places boggy

[1] South Fork of the Owyhee River. This site is now occupied by Wild Horse Reservoir.

[2] At this point in the manuscript there is an insert mark. Above it the words "though this valley is not known to have ever been hunted" are interlineated. The phrase would be more appropriate following the preceding sentence.

the snow having but very recently gone off the ground indeed we passed over several banks of it.

Satdy 2. Fine weather. We are like to be devoured with Musquitoes. Did not raise camp that we might see what beaver might be taken. The people visited & changed their traps. Only 12 beaver was taken which is nothing for the number of traps *about 150* which were in the water, and what is worse the men complain there is little signs of any more worth while being got. Several of the people were out hunting but with little success which I regret as provisions are getting very scarce in the camp. Not an animal to be seen but Antelopes and but few of them and even these are so shy that it is difficult to approach them. There are some cranes in the valley, but almost as difficult to be got at as the Antelopes. The hunters observe the tracks of some sheep in the Mountains but they appear to have been driven off by some straggling Indians whose tracks are seen. All together this is a very poor country. Owing to the lateness of the spring the Indians who frequent these parts to collect roots have not yet assembled so that even a few roots bad as they are are not to be got to assist those who are scarce of food.

Sundy 3. Cloudy fine weather. Continued our journey 12 Miles S. S. W. to a branch of Ogden's river where it issues from a steep snow covered mountain.[3] This stream is well wooded with poplar and willows and appears well adapted for beaver yet the people found only one solitary lodge on it and scarcely a mark of beaver either old or new, though they examined it for a considerable distance.[4] One man set a few traps. Seven of

[3] North Fork of the Humboldt River. The mountain is one of a rugged chain, the Independence Mountains.

[4] Seeing this country for the first time, Work did not realize that most of these streams are intermittent despite the growth of trees and willows along the courses. In normal years they will be dry from mid-June until the fall rains or, lacking them, the spring run-off.

the Men A. Finlay, P. Finlay, M. Finlay, M. Plante, A. Plante, Bt. Gardipie, and Soteaux St. Germain, separated from the party this morning in order to proceed down the river if practicable and thence by the usual road to the fort by Snake river,[5] and endeavour to pick up a few beaver by the way, but principally to procure some animals to subsist on. These men are all half Indians, some of them with large families, and placing too much reliance on their capability as hunters did not take so much precaution as the other men to provide a stock of food previous to leaving the buffalo. they are therefore now entirely out of provisions and it is expected they will have a better chance of killing Antelopes & chivereau when only a few than when the camp are altogether.[6]

7 Beaver were taken this morning. Making 19 in all this valley where we expected to make a good hunt.

Mondy 4. Very stormy cold weather. Crossed the Mountains a distance of 18 Miles S. S. W. to a small stream which fals [*sic*] into the W. branch of Sandwich island river. The road very hilly and rugged & in places stony. we had several banks of snow to pass the road in places nearly barred with fallen wood. The little fork where we are encamped is well wooded with poplar and willows, yet only in two places are the mark of a beaver to be seen. Some of the men have proceeded on to the main branch and set 22 traps, where they saw the appearance of some beaver.

Tuesdy 5. Stormy cold weather. Continued our route 9 Miles

[5] The party was directed to proceed down the South Fork to the Owyhee and thence to the Snake River. It would follow the Snake to near Huntington, Oregon, where it would strike the route taken by the brigade on its outward march from Fort Nez Perces.

[6] Earlier entries indicate that Work was happy to be relieved of the burden of directing this group. The difficulty of feeding both horses and people in the country immediately ahead of him made this decrease in size an intelligent move, as subsequent entries will indicate.

S. S. W. to the main branch of the river the road hilly and rugged. Crossed a small stream with a number of hot springs on its banks, some of them near a boiling temperature.[7] The river here has been lately very high & overflowed its banks but the waters are subsiding & *river about 10 yards wide* have fallen a good deal. The traps which were set yesterday produced only 6 beaver. The men were out in every direction setting their traps, and complain that there is very little appearance of beaver. This seems to be a miserably poor country not even an antelope to be seen in the plains. The tracks of some sheep are to be seen in the Mountains but they are so shy there is no approaching them.

Some Indians visited our camp this morning and traded a few roots but the quantity was very small.

Wedy 6. Stormy cold weather. Did not raise camp. The men out in different directions with their traps. Those which were in the water yesterday produced 14 beaver. The men begin to have a little more expectations. The Indians stole two traps in the night, one from Kanota & 1 from A. Hoole. There is no means of pursuing or finding out the thief as they run to the mountains. There is little doubt they came to attempt stealing the horses but not finding an opportunity they fell in with & carried off the traps.

Thursdy 7. Still raw cold weather, blowing fresh.

Did not move camp. 10 beaver were taken. Some of the people went with their traps to some small streams which fall in from the Eastward which was not hunted by Mr. Ogden's people when they hunted this river two years ago. they saw the appearance of a few beaver but nothing for a new place.

---

[7] The stream is variously called the South Fork and the East Fork of the Owyhee. The creek with the hot springs is Jack Creek. The camp this night would have been on the river northeast of the present Tuscarora, Nevada.

Friday 8. Weather milder than these days past. Moved a few miles down the river, to a better location for the horses where we will be a little nearer the people with their traps. 17 Beaver were taken. Some of the people moved their traps a little farther down the river. The road is very hilly, rugged, & stony. Some Indians visited our camp this morning with a few roots.

Satdy 9. Did not raise camp. The people visited and changed their traps. 7 beaver were taken. Some of the men have not returned from the traps.

Sundy 10. Cloudy cold weather. Did not move camp. 18 beaver were taken. 2 traps stolen from Pichette & *1 from Aubichon.* The men who went farthest down the river returned, and report there are but small signs of beaver. those from the forks to the Eastward say there are few there. Some Indians visited us with a few roots to trade. Miserably poor as these wretches are and the small quantity of roots they bring yet it furnishes several of the people with a meal, occasionally, which is very acceptable to them as provisions, previous to the late supply of beaver was becoming very scarce among us.

Mondy 11. Warm fine weather. Did not move camp. 7 beaver were taken. There are still a chance beaver in the little forks to the Eastward and down the river towards the rocks,[8] (where the river bears so rapidly that no beaver are to be found,) but not enough to employ all the people, or worth while to delay for, the season being so far advanced. We therefore intend to move up the river tomorrow and hunt the head of it.

Tuesdy 12. Cloudy sultry weather in the morning which was

[8] West of Whiterock, Nevada.

succeeded by thunder and heavy rain & hail, raw cold weather afternoon. Raised camp and marched 7 Miles up the river where we had to encamp with the bad weather. 6 beaver were taken, 2 traps stolen one from Pichette & 1 from Rocque.

Wedy 13. Overcast blowing fresh towards evening. Proceeded up the river 11 Miles S. S. E. to opposite a branch which falls in from the Eastward. here the Trappers with Mr. Ogden crossed the mountains from Ogden's river to this place two years ago.[9] I meant to have taken the same road but have altered the plan by it being represented to me that several days will be saved & some bad stony road avoided by crossing the mountains farther to the Southward, & falling upon Ogden's river farther down. In the part of the river we will miss there are few beaver to be expected. Some of the men visited the head of this river to the mountain, and two forks which fall in from the Eastward to near the source and though they are well wooded & apparently well adapted for beaver, yet scarcely a mark of one is to be seen.

Thursdy 14. Fine weather. Continued our journey 18 Miles across the Mountains; viz: S. W. 9 miles to the top of the mountains, & 9 miles down the S. side of the mountains. The road hilly and uneven & in places stony. The mountains though not high have still patches of snow here and there upon them. Some of the people were out hunting but without success. A chance Antelope is the only animal to be seen and these are so shy that it is very difficult to approach them. The hunters saw three Indians, and the men who were on discovery yesterday, saw some more, and their tracks are to be seen in every direction yet none of them visit our camp.

[9] This point is near the present junction of State Highways 11 and 18. Ogden must have followed the route now taken by Highway 11 from the North Fork of the Humboldt.

Friday 15. Fine warm weather. Did not raise camp on account of one of the women being brought to bed. Some of the people were out hunting but without success.

Satdy 16. Fine weather. Continued our route 12 Miles S. over a number of hills & valleys to a small river where we encamped for the night.[10] The road good but here and there stony & generally gravelly, & hard which much wears down the horses hoofs and renders their feet sore. These nights past we had sharp frost, but here the weather is sultry and we are annoyed with Musquitoes which will neither give ourselves peace nor allow the poor horses to feed.

Sundy 17. Fine warm weather. Marched 21 Miles S. S. W. along the W side of an extensive plain to near Ogden's river, the plain here is partially overflowed and become a swamp.[11] We could scarcely find a spot to encamp, among the lodges the horses are nearly bogging, and to mend the matter we are like to be devoured by innumberable swarms of musquitoes, which do not allow us a moments tranquility, and so torment the horses that notwithstanding their long day's march, they cannot feed. All hands are ahead of the camp with their traps but found the river so high, having overflowed its banks that they could not approach it except in chance places. three of the men set 9 traps which were all that could be put in the water. I much regret finding the river so high that it cannot be hunted, As the people's last reliance was upon the few beaver which they expected to take in it, in order to make up their hunt but more particularly for food. The most of them are becoming very scarce of provisions and they have now no other resource but to kill horses. Some of the people nearly devoured their horses crossing the swamp on their way to the camp. They saw a small

10 The camp would be on Maggie Creek north of Carlin, Nevada.
11 The plain would be the flats west of Carlin, Nevada.

herd of Antelopes in the plain but they could not be approached. A few wild fowl were killed, of which there are a good many in the swamp.

Mondy 18. Cloudy warm sultry weather. Pursued our journey 14 Miles S. S. W. & 7 Miles W. down the river.[12] Marched longer today than we intended not being able to find a place to encamp in consequence of the swampiness of the banks of the river which are almost everywhere overflowed. The men were out along the river with their traps but not one could be set. Only one beaver was taken in the 9 which were set yesterday. It is the opinion of the more experienced hunters, that there are a few beaver still in this part of the river, but owing to the height of the water they cannot be taken. People passed twice this way about this season of the year before but never saw the water so high as at present. We expected to have found some Indians here and obtained some eatables from them either roots or one thing or another, but none are to be seen in consequence of the height of the water. they cannot remain on the river but are off in the Mountains.

Tuesdy 19. Clear very warm weather. Continued our journcy 18 Miles down the river which here runs to the N. W.[13] The river is still full to the banks and all the low places overflowed. The men again visited the river but could not put a trap in the water. Both people & horses are like to be devoured by innumerable swarms of Musquitoes & sandflies. The horses cannot feed they are so annoyed by them. The banks of the river are so swampy that they bog when they approach to drink.

Wedy 20. Overcast, Thunder and very heavy rain afternoon. Continued our journey 19 Miles N. W. along the river & thence

---

[12] The camp would be east of Beowawe, Nevada.
[13] This would put the party northwest of Battle Mountain.

to the foot of the mountains where we found a little water and some grass for the horses.[14] These three days the river runs through an extensive plain here the Mountains approach close to it. The farther we descend the river it becomes the more difficult to approach it on account of its banks being overflowed. Two of the Men, J. Toupin & G. Rocque each killed a horse having nothing to eat their provisions being all done. On leaving the buffalo the people calculated upon getting a few beaver and did not lay in such a stock of provisions as they otherwise would have done. This is really a miserable poor country. Not even an Antelope to be seen.

Thursdy 21. Cloudy fine weather, blowing fresh in the morning. Proceeded across the mountain and then across an extensive plain 20 Miles W. to a small fork which falls into Ogden's river,[15] by this route we save 2 days journey besides going round by the river. To our great disappointment and contrary to our expectations we found the little river overflowed its banks and the plain in its neighbourhood is a swamp so that we could not approach it. it is to be apprehended we will have much trouble crossing it. The different parties which formerly passed this way found this creek with very little water in it. Several of the people were out hunting but did not see an animal. They expected to find some Antelopes in the hills.

Friday 22. Warm sultry weather. Proceeded up the river 20 Miles N. N. W., and succeeded in crossing it by a bridge of willows. The river here is narrow but very deep with clayey banks so steep & soft that the horses could not get out of it were

---

[14] The camp would be on the east side of the spur running south from Adams Peak, northeast of Golconda, Nevada. This day's march marks the beginning of the move north to Fort Nez Perces.

[15] The Little Humboldt River. The brigade is about fifteen miles north of Winnemuca, Nevada.

they thrown in to swim across. To near this place its banks were so overflowed that it could not be approached. This was a hard days work both on people and horses. The horses as well as people are like to be devoured by swarms of Musquitoes and gadflies. The river here is well wooded and seems remarkably well adapted for beaver yet there is not the least mark of one to be seen in it.

Satdy 23. Fine warm weather. Continued our journey 15 Miles W. N. W. across the plain to the foot of the mountains. we crossed two other forks of the same river we left in the morning, one of them much larger than it but we found a good ford.[16] Some Indians were seen along the mountains but they fled on our approach.

Sundy 24. Clear fine weather. Crossed the Mountains 19 Miles W. N. W.[17] Road very hilly & stony from the steepness & height of the Mountain and the badness of the road. this was a most harrassing and fatiguing day on both men & horses. The first tracks of Indians seen but none of them approached us. The best hunters of the party were out in the Mountains, (which has still a good deal of snow on it,) in quest of sheep, but without success. They saw the tracks of some, but could not find them.

Mondy 25. Clear warm weather. Marched 7 Miles N. N. E. along the foot of the Mountain and 15 Miles across the plain to a little river,[18] which runs to the Southward, and which we found impassable, its banks having been lately overflowed, and

[16] The brigade is now moving away from the flooded bottom lands in the hope of making a hunt on the small streams in the mountains. The creeks are Martin Creek and an unnamed stream.

[17] The camp would be near, but to the northeast of, the junction of U.S. 95 and State Highway 8A.

[18] The river is Quinn River and the camp would be southwest of Orovada. It is doubtful that this stretch of river would support beaver in ordinary years.

remain still like a quagmire. The best hunters were out but as usual did not see a single animal of any sort. One of the men P. Bernie was under the necessity of killing one of his horses to eat. Thus are the people in this miserably poor country obliged to kill and feed upon those useful animals the companions of their labours. We passed a small Indian camp, but the poor frightened wretches fled on our approach and concealed themselves among the wormwood. Only two of the men who were ahead saw any of them.

Tuesdy 26. Very warm sultry weather. Marched 5 miles N. up the river to a place where we crossed one of its forks with little trouble, but the other which was close too was very difficult. the men had to wade across it with the baggage, its banks are like a morass and several of the horses bogged so that they had to be dragged out. Crossed a plain 5 miles N. N. W. to another fork which we crossed without further difficulty than bogging a few of the horses.[19] This was a most harrassing & fatiguing day both on men & horses.

Wedy 27. Blowing fresh, yet very warm weather. Continued our route 15 Miles N. W. along the foot of the Mountains to a small rivulet which falls into the river we passed yesterday.[20] The road good but in places stony & embarrassed with wormwood. The hunters were out today but without success. Two Antelopes were seen yesterday, which was a novelty.

Thursdy 28. Very warm weather though blowing fresh the afterpart of the day. Proceeded on our journey 23 Miles N. W.

[19] The first of the streams would be Rebel Creek. The other two are unnamed.

[20] This stream is designated as Quinn River on a sign of the highway bridge but not on the maps. The brigade passed the site of McDermitt, Nevada, and passed into Oregon on this day.

along the foot of the Mountains, crossed the head of the river we left two days ago, and over a hill to a small rivulet which is said to be a fork of the Owyhee river.²¹ The road good but in places stony.

The hunters were out, F. Payette had the good fortune to kill a Male Antelope. One of the men saw four sheep in the plain but did not kill any of them.

Friday 29. Blowing fresh, which rendered the weather a little cool and pleasant. Marched 28 miles N. N. W. first across a plain and salt swamp and over a range of hills and across another valley part of which has the appearance of the bed of a lake but is quite dry & hard & finally a swamp & encamped near the foot of the Mountain covered with snow.²² The road in places stony and from the length of the encampment, very fatiguing both on horses & people, neither of which have a moments quietness either to feed or repose, they are so annoyed with innumerable swarms of Musquitoes. The hunters were out but without success, they saw the tracks of some Antelopes and sheep. Some Indian tracks fresh were seen but none of them approached us, some of them had horses.

Satdy 30. Warm & very sultry in the morning, a breeze of wind afterwards. Continued our journey along the foot of the Mountains 18 miles N. by W. The road good, passed two small lakes in one of which the people found a good many eggs.²³ L. Kanota killed an Antelope and F. Payette a young one. A. Letendre had to kill one of his horses to eat.

²¹ An unnamed, intermittent stream.

²² The party passed south of Crooked Creek Springs, across a spur of the Sheepshead Mountains, and camped north of Manns Lake at the foot of the Steens Mountains.

²³ The two lakes are Juniper and Ten Cent lakes. The camp would be near State Highway 78 at the foot of the mountain.

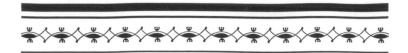

July, 1831

Sundy 1. Fine weather. Our road lay along the foot of the mountains 10 Miles N. & W. and thence across the mountains 12 Miles N. W. Part of the road hilly and very stony. The stony road *& continual mounting* are wearing out the horses hoofs and rendering them lame. Though the mountains in our neighbourhood have still patches of snow on them, the little creek where we are encamped barely affords sufficient water for the horses to drink.[1] The hunters killed nothing today. J. Despard killed one of his horses.

Mondy 2. Fine weather. Continued our journey N. W. 19 Miles to Sylvaille's Lake,[2] the road part of the day stony. The lake unusually high and the water brackish and so very bad that it is like a vomit to drink it. The hunters were out but without success. There are a number of wildfowl in the lake but they are so shy that they cannot be approached.

Tuesdy 3. Warm sultry weather. *A thunder storm in the evening.* Our road lay along the lake and across a point to Syl-

[1] The small stream that flows beside State Highway 78 at the foot of the mountain.

[2] Malheur Lake. The brigade camped just north of the present site of the Malheur National Wild Life Refuge headquarters. Actual sites by the lakes are nearly impossible to identify, as much of the lake bed has been drained and planted.

vaille's river in rather a circuitous road nearly W. N. W. 20 miles.[3] The road good. Some of the men set a few traps, they saw the appearance of a chance beaver.

Wedy 4. Very warm but blowing fresh afternoon. Continued our journey up the river 15 miles N. N. W. to the first rocks.[4] The horses like to be devoured by gadflies. F. Payette went to hunt yesterday & returned today with two Antelopes. L. Kanota also killed two. The traps which were set yesterday produced 4 beaver.

Thursdy 5. Very warm weather. Did not raise camp in order to allow the horses to repose, of which they are in much need. they have marched 19 days successively without stopping a day to rest. they have been becoming lean for some time back and their hoofs are so much worn that some of them are becoming lame. The most of the people set their traps yesterday. 13 beaver were taken.

The hunters were out. A Hoole killed a Chivereau and the Boy Peerish an Antelope. Four Indians paid us a visit, they had nothing with them to trade. they received a few trifles and promised to return with some roots to trade.

Fridy 6. Fine weather. Marched about 28 Miles N. N. W. across a point & fell again upon the river by this road.[5] it is shorter than following all the turns of the river. The people out with their traps. 5 beaver and 1 Otter taken. In the morning one of the men arrived with a load of young herons. he found a place where they are very numerous. Some more of

---

[3] Now Silvies River, a corruption of *Sylvailles*. It was named for Antoine Sylvaille, a freeman with the Ogden party of 1826–27, who was drowned at The Dalles in 1830. The camp would be just west of Lawen.

[4] Northwest of Burns, Oregon. The point is still unmistakable.

[5] The route probably took the party to the mouth of Trout Creek.

the people who we[re] short of food immediately went to get a supply. These birds are very fat, some of the people say that [they] are scarcely eatable. Some of the people went off to hunt & have not yet returned.

Satdy 7. Fine weather. Continued our journey 20 miles up the river N. N. W.[6] Road stony hilly & uneven. 5 beaver taken. The hunters arrived. A. Hoole killed an elk and 2 black tail Chivereau & the Boy Peerish 1 young elk. The men with the camp caught a wounded deer away up the river.

Sundy 8. Fine weather. Proceeded up the river 15 Miles N. N. W. to the head of the second valley.[7] 2 beaver were taken. Some Antelopes were seen crossing the valley but none killed.

Mondy 9. Fine warm weather, blowing fresh afternoon.
Left the river, which is enclosed by steep hills and struck across the hills and fell upon the river at the head of the upper valley at the foot of the mountains, a distance of 13 Miles N. W.[8] The road good. The hills we passed in the morning well timbered with lofty pine, the vally is clear of wood except some willows along the different forks of the river. The hunters were out. A. Hoole killed an Antelope, and T. Tewatcon a Chivereau.

Tuesdy 10. Very warm weather, still a breeze of wind in the after part of the day. Crossed the Mountains to Day's river a distance of 22 miles N. W.[9] The road very hilly and steep particularly the N. side of the Mountain. The mountain is

[6] This camp site would be just south of Seneca, Oregon.
[7] The camp would be near the mouth of Scotty Creek.
[8] The point is unmistakable though there is no geographic place name to give it.
[9] John Day River. They followed the ridge lines and apparently reached the stream about a dozen miles below the town of John Day, Oregon.

thickly wooded with tall pine timber. both people and horses much fatigued on reaching the camp. part of the road stony. Day's river is well wooded with poplar & willows. Two Indians visited our camp this morning and traded 5 beaver.

Wedy 11. Very warm sultry weather. Proceeded down the river 16 miles W.[10] Parts of the road hilly and stony, and very fatiguing on the horses several of whom gave up on the way and with difficulty reached the camp.

Some of the men set a few traps yesterday and took two beaver this morning.

Thursdy 12. Very warm weather. Continued our route down the river,[11] which still runs to the Westward 11 Miles when we stopped near a camp of Snake Indians who have the river barred across for the purpose of catching salmon. We with difficulty obtained a few salmon from them, perhaps enough to give all hands a meal. they are taking but very few salmon and complain of being hungry themselves. No roots can be obtained from them, but some of the men traded two or three dogs, but even the few of these animals they have are very lean always a sign of a scarcity of food among Indians. We found two horses with these people who were stolen from the men which I left on Snake River in September last.[12] they gave up the horses without hesitation and said that they received them from another band that are in the mountains with some more horses, which were stolen at the same time. it appears from their account that early in the spring some Snakes stole 13 horses from these men at the same time and immediately made their

[10] This camp would be near the present town of Daysville, Oregon.

[11] In order to reconcile the journal distances from this point to Fort Nez Perces, it must be assumed that Work is mistaken in the direction of the river at this point. He would be heading north towards Kimberly, Oregon.

[12] Alexander Carson and party. They had separated from the brigade on September 7, 1830.

way to this quarter with them. The uncertainty of finding the Indians with the rest of the horses in the mountains, the fatigued state of our horses, the advanced state of the season and above all the scarcity of food among the people, deters me from sending some men in search of these horses. I however offered the Indians a reward if they would go and bring them. I also gave them a little remuneration for the two they had here. Part of the way today the road lay over rugged rocks on the bank of the river[13] and was very hard on the already wounded feet of the horses. 5 beaver were taken in the morning.

Fridy 13. Fine weather. Did not raise camp in order to repose the horses feet a little. Only 3 or 4 Salmon could be obtained from the Indians. They complain of being starved themselves. 1 beaver was taken.

Satdy 14. Cool pleasant weather. Continued our journey down the river 25 Miles W. The road hilly and stony. The horses jaded & the people exhausted on reaching the encampment. Only 3 or 4 Salmon could be obtained from the Indians in the morning before we started.

Sundy 15. Fine cool weather. Continued our course W. 8 miles down the river to another fork which falls in from the North, up which we proceeded 7 Miles.[14] The road continued hilly and stony. These two days the people found great quantities of currants along the banks of the river.

Mondy 16. Fine weather. Proceeded 8 Miles N. E. up the

13 This day's journey would take the party to a point just downstream from Kimberly, Oregon.
14 Work must mean the North Fork of the John Day River, which comes in from the northeast.

river, when we took a Northern direction for 11 Miles across the Mountains,[15] which was here thickly wooded. the road in places stony and very hilly and unev[en], and very fatiguing on both men and horses. The hunters were out but without success except one deer which F. Payette killed. Unfortunately we have but very indifferent feeding for the horses after the hard days work.

Tuesdy 17. Fine weather. Continued our journey across the mountains 25 miles N. W.[16] The country the same in appearance as yesterday until we got out of the woods in the after part of the day when the road lay over a number of naked stony hills the length of the days journey and the badness of the road rendered this a harrassing day both on men and horses. Some fresh tracks of red deer were seen in the course of the day but they could not be come up with.

Wedy 18. Cool in the morning but very sultry warm weather afterwards. Proceeded ahead of the camp early in the morning accompanied by seven men and arrived at Fort Nezperces in the afternoon. Mainly through there being soft sand during the heat of the day excessively oppressive on the horses as well as the riders.

Thursdy 19. Stormy but warm weather. The different parties who separated from the camp have arrived, Plante & Party[17] yesterday the others some time ago. The party whom I left in September had the misfortune to lose the whole of their horses, nearly 30 in number, early in the spring. they imprudently

[15] The road would follow the North Fork of the John Day past Monument, Oregon. The party then struck across country toward Pilot Rock.

[16] This camp would be near Pilot Rock, Oregon.

[17] Charles Plante and seven others who left the brigade on May 12, 1831.

allowed them to stray a short distance from the camp when three or four Indians in the evening about sunset.[18] The loss was the result of a great degree of negligence on the part of the men. They also put what few skins they had with other articles in cache where the Indians found them carried off from a pack to a pack and a half[19] of the few beaver they had. The half breeds lost two of the horses by theft, and made but very few skins. Plant & Party also found very few beaver, but they lost no horses.

Fridy 20. Fine weather. The people whom I left two days ago arrived safe. Since our spring journey commenced we have travelled upwards of 1000 miles and from the height of the water and the scarcity of beaver we have very little for the labour and trouble which we experienced. Previous to taking up our winter quarters last fall we traveled upwards of 980 miles which with the different moves made during the winter makes better than 2000 miles travelled during our voyage.

Total loss of horses during the voyage   82

viz:

Stolen by the Blackfeet when P. L Etang killed			3	
do.	Snake Indians from A. Carson & party		22	
do.	do.	from my party during winter	3	
do.	do.	from the Half breeds in summer after leaving me	2	30

---

[18] Work was obviously irritated when he wrote this passage and, thus, did not notice that he failed to complete the sentence. The party referred to is the Alexander Carson party which had separated from the brigade on September 7, 1830. On the stolen horses, see July 12 above.

[19] "Each pack weighs ninety pounds, and contains on an average from fifty to sixty beaver-skins" (Ross Cox, *The Columbia River*, 194).

Died or gave up on the way previous to reaching
the three hill plain in the fall, 1 by Toupin,
1 by Dumais, & 3 by the Half breeds when they
left the party on Salmon river 5

Died, or left crossing the plain in the fall 26

Died during the winter 11 42

Killed for food by   A Carson & party 3
 do.   do. My party during summer 5
 do.   do. C. Plants party   do. 1 9

Drowned crossing a river by Rocque 1

       Total 82

Appendix A:

The Personnel of Work's Brigade

Aubichon, Baptiste. (Also Obichon. Both spellings are to be found in company records). A native of the parish of Sorel, Canada, he was with Work on the 1832–33 expedition to California. He settled in the Willamette Valley, and his marriage is recorded on May 3, 1839.[1]

Baptiste, Joseph J. He was one of the freemen with this expedition and was with Work again the following year. He had been in the Pacific Northwest for a number of years, most of his service having been with the Snake Country brigades.[2]

Bercier, Pierre. He had been with Ogden in 1826–27. At the time of this brigade he was listed in company records as fifty-one years of age and a native of Berthier parish. This was his thirtieth year of service in the fur trade.[3] A stream in Camas Prairie bore his name, which would indicate that he had been a member of earlier Snake Country expeditions.

Birnie, P. He was with Work again in 1831–32. In the following year he was attached to the Laframboise section of the Bona-

---

[1] Maloney, Alice B., ed., *Fur Brigade to Bonaventura*, 103, hereafter cited as Maloney, *Bonaventura*; Nichols, *Mantle*, 286.

[2] B 202/a/11, March 25, 1832.

[3] *HBRS*, XXIII, 2. See above, October 12, 1830.

ventura brigade. He died in the Umpqua Mountains on September 28, 1833.[4]

Carson, Alexander. Having come overland with the Wilson Price Hunt party in 1810, he and three others were left on Mad River to trap in 1811. He remained in the country as a trapper for a good many years, and was with Ogden in the Snake Country in 1824–25, deserting to the Americans on May 24, 1825. He was, evidently, back with Ogden again in 1829–30. He is not listed with the 1831–32 party but was with Laframboise in 1832–33. He was killed by the Indians in Yamhill County, Oregon, in 1835.[5]

Champaigne, François. (Or Champagne.) He was then thirty years of age and had come from the parish of Lenoure. This was his tenth year of service in the fur trade, most of it in the Pacific Northwest. He was with Ogden in 1826–27.[6] He had begun his service in the Northwest at Fort George. He was with Work again in 1831–32 and in 1832–33, and in 1834 he was on the Umpqua expedition. He retired from company service in 1841 and became a Willamette Valley settler.[7]

Cloutier, Jérôme. He was a freeman with this brigade. He had also been with Ogden in 1826–27. He was killed by the Blackfeet while with Work in the fall of 1831.[8]

Depot, Pierre. He was from St. Roch parish, District of Mon-

[4] Maloney, *Bonaventura*, 105.
[5] Maloney, "Alexander Carson, Wilhamot Freeman," *OHQ*, XXXIX (1938), 16 ff., *HBRS*, XXIII, 2, 234; appendix B, below; Maloney, *Bonaventura*, 104.
[6] *HBRS*, XXIII, 2; B 76/d/10, p. 17; Maloney, *Bonaventura*, 100–101; B 223/g/6, f. 9.
[7] B 223/g/6, f. 9; B 202/a/11, January 26, 1832.
[8] *HBRS*, XXIII, 2; John Work, Field Journal, 1831–32, October 31, 1831.

treal. He had been with Ogden in 1824–25 and was attacked by a grizzly while setting his traps on May 3, 1825. He was with Ogden in 1826–27 as a freeman. He retired to become a farmer in the Willamette Valley and married a Klamath Indian woman.[9]

Desland, Jean. He was with Work again on the 1831–32 brigade. He was seriously wounded in one of the encounters with the Blackfeet on November 24, 1831.[10]

Despard, Joseph. Church records list him as from St. Hyacinthe, District of Montreal, while company records list him as being from Yamaska parish. He was thirty-six years of age and in his fourteenth year of service at the time of this expedition. Previous experience included the Snake Country expeditions of 1825–26 and 1826–27. He was reported to have killed a slave on December 11, 1825, while with Ogden. He married a Chinook Indian woman on January 21, 1839, and legitimatized several children at that time. One of them, a boy of eleven, may have been one of the children of the 1830–31 party.[11]

Dubruille, Jean Baptiste. From St. Anne, Montreal Island, he had served with the Pacific Fur Company and was one of those listed as transferring to the Northwest Company service in 1813. At that time he was listed as one of the servants at Flathead House. He was with Alexander R. McLeod on the 1828 expedition to the Umpqua to recover Jedediah Smith's furs. His Snake Country experience included the brigades of 1825–

[9] Nichols, *Mantle*, 265, 321; *HBRS*, XIII, 231; *HBRS*, XXIII, 2.
[10] Work, Field Journal, 1831–32.
[11] *HBRS*, XXIII, 2; T. C. Elliott, ed., "Journal of John Work, November and December, 1824," *Washington Historical Quarterly*, III (1912), 200; *HBRS*, XIII, 103–104.

26, 1830–31, and 1831–32. He was also with the Bonaventura brigade of 1832–33 and remained a member of it through 1834. He retired to the Willamette as a settler and was married to an Indian woman on July 9, 1839. He died sometime prior to April 2, 1861.[12]

Dumais, A. He was with Work again on the 1831–32 brigade. He was drowned in the Snake River on July 19, 1832, as the party was returning to Fort Nez Perces.[13]

Finlay, Augustin. He had been with Ogden in 1829–30. He was with Work again in 1831–32 and is mentioned several times in the journal.[14] He and the other Finlays in the party seem to have been brothers, and it is quite possible that they were the sons of the famous Jacques Rafael "Jacco" Finlay.

Finlay, Miquam. After starting with the 1831–32 brigade, he deserted it on October 24, 1831.[15]

Finlay, Pinesta. He was with the Flathead Indians in the fall of 1831. He visited Work's camp October 23, 1831, and departed the following day with four members of the brigade for the Indian camp.

Gardipie, Baptiste. He was with Work again in 1831–32 and the Bonaventura brigade of 1832–33. In 1846 he acted as a guide for two emigrant parties to California.[16]

[12] Nichols, *Mantle*, 270, 314; F 4/61; *HBRS*, XXIII, 176n.; B 202/a/11, January 26, 1832.

[13] B 202/a/11, p. 68.

[14] Barker, *McLoughlin Letters*, 128; Work, Field Journal, 1831–32.

[15] Work, Field Journal, 1831–32. The Journal is also the source of information about Pinesta Finlay.

[16] Maloney, *Bonaventura*, 101.

Hoole, Antoine. He started with the 1831–32 brigade but was left at Fort Nez Perces on September 9, 1831, because of illness. He had several years of service in the Inland Empire, much of it at posts.[17]

Indian, Pichette's brother-in-law. He may have been one of the youths listed as able to bear arms.[18]

Indian, Kanota's slave. He was probably one of the men counted by Work as able to bear arms. He was not with Kanota and he was armed when he was killed by the Blackfeet.[19] This fact is not surprising. Slaves of company servants were seldom freed, as that freedom made them liable to immediate enslavement by the Indians, but they were free except in this technical sense.

Kanota, Louis. A Nippesing Indian, according to Work, he had been with Ogden in the Snake Country in 1824–25, deserting to the Americans with his furs on May 24, 1825. He was with Work again in 1831–32[20] and was also a member of the 1832–33 brigade. In 1835 he was listed as employed at Fort Colville, where he was waiting for James Douglas to return from the Council of the Northern Department. He was still on the roll at Fort Colville in 1838.[21]

La Forte, Michel. From St. Hyacinthe, District of Montreal, he was with Ogden in the Snake Country in 1824–25 and again in 1826–27. He was with John Work again in 1831–32 and 1832–33. He gave his occupation as *engagé* when he was

---

[17] Work, Field Journal, 1831–32; B 146/a/2, p. 18.

[18] See August 22, 1830, above.

[19] See August 22 and September 25, 1830, above.

[20] See April 17, 1831, above; *HBRS*, XIII, 234.

[21] Maloney, *Bonaventura*, 103; Walter N. Sage, *Sir James Douglas and British Columbia*, 84–85; Nichols, *Mantle*, 261.

married in 1839. At that time he had three children old enough to have been with the brigade of 1830–31.[22]

L'Etang, Pierre. He engaged for three years in the Columbia Department in 1818 at Rivière-du-Loup. He was with Work as a guide (in charge of a boat) in 1825 and served in the same capacity with David Douglas in the following year, when the naturalist was gathering materials in the Northwest. In November, 1828, he was with the McLeod expedition to recover Jedediah Smith's furs. He was an *engagé* for the year 1829–30, and following that engagement, he joined the Snake Country brigade. He was killed by the Blackfeet on September 25, 1830. John McLoughlin, reporting L'Etang's death to Governor Simpson, paid the Canadian high tribute, saying "by whose death we have lost one of the best Men in this department."[23]

Le Tendre, Antoine. Engaged in 1812 from Sorel, Canada, he is found on the roster of the Snake Country expedition of 1824–25. He was with Work in the fall of 1831 and was killed by the Blackfeet on October 31 while out looking at his traps.[24]

Longtain, André. (Also Lonctain.) He was from the parish of St. Constant, District of Montreal, according to one account. Company records list him as from St. Pierre parish. He was a veteran of a number of years' varied service in the Pacific Northwest and this was his tenth year with the company. He was thirty-four years of age and had served in the Snake Country with Ogden in 1826–27. He was with Work again in 1831–32

---

[22] Nichols, *Mantle*, 266; *HBRS*, XIII, 3; *HBRS*, XXIII, 2; Maloney, *Bonaventura*, 102.

[23] Francis D. Haines, Jr., "Death of a Snake Country Trapper: Pierre L'Etang," *OHQ*, LVI (1955), 248–54.

[24] Quebec, *Rapport de L'Archiviste . . . de Quebec . . . 1945–1946*, 325; *HBRS*, XIII, 3; Work, Field Journal, 1831–32, October 31, 1831.

and the Bonaventura brigade in 1832–33. He retired to became a Willamette settler, where he raised a large family
and was still living in 1858.[25] Active in community affairs,
Longtain appears to have been a leader. His name was on a
petition to Congress attacking Hudson's Bay Company and
asking for protection by the American government. He later
wrote to McLoughlin apologizing to him and stating that the
petition had been misrepresented to him.[26]

Majeau, A. Having served with the company for several years
before 1830, he was with Work again in 1831–32 and again
with the Bonaventura brigade of 1832–33.[27] His name has been
incorrectly transcribed as *Masseau,* the *j* being read as *ss.*

Payette, François. His first engagement in the fur trade seems
to have been for one year at Baye Quinte. His home is given as
the parish of St. Roc. Following the first engagement, which
apparently ended in May, 1811, he seems to have engaged with
the Pacific Fur Company. He came to the Pacific Northwest on
Astor's supply ship, the *Beaver* and was on the roster of men
transferred from the Pacific Fur Company to the Northwest
Company in 1813. His name appears on the roster of em-
ployees in 1814 at Fort George. He was with Donald McKenzie on the Snake Country expedition of 1818. He may have
been on subsequent Snake Country expeditions, but he was employed at Spokane House in 1822. He was with Ogden on the
Snake Country expeditions from 1824 through 1828.

Payette was not with Ogden in 1829–30 but returned to the

[25] Nichols, *Mantle,* 264, 311; *HBRS,* XXIII, 2; Maloney, *Bonaventura,*
102.
[26] A copy of the petition and the McLoughlin letter are in the Archives
of Hudson's Bay Company.
[27] Maloney, *Bonaventura,* 102. On the spelling of the name, Work did
use the *ss* letter but shaped it differently. This is a *j* beyond any shadow of
a doubt.

Snake Country brigade as second-in-command to Work in 1830. He served in the same capacity with the 1831–32 expedition and was to have continued in this capacity in the Bonaventura brigade of 1832–33 but had to be left behind at Fort Vancouver because of illness. He engaged for three years in the grade of interpreter in 1833 and again in 1836. In 1837 he became post master of Fort Boise and retained that position until his retirement in 1844. It was while serving at Fort Boise that he became a well-known figure to the travelers on the Oregon Trail, many of whom mention him favorably. Payette retired to Canada in 1844 and disappeared without a trace in 1845, leaving a substantial credit in his account with the company.[28]

Peerish, Boy. He was probably the son of *engagé* Pierre Martineau who was stationed at Fort Nez Perces at the time the expedition set out. Martineau was usually referred to as "Pierriche" by the writers of the Fort Nez Perces journals. It would not be illogical that Work, who was not fluent in French, would render *Pierriche* as *Peerish*. He was with Work again in 1832–33, and he may be the Little Pierre mentioned by McLoughlin in a letter to Michel Laframboise in April, 1832.[29]

Pichette, Louis. From the parish of St. Onis, Montreal, he left Canada in 1817 and arrived at Fort George the following year. He is not mentioned in the earlier Snake Country journals nor is his name to be found in the published version of the 1831–32 journal of John Work. He was, however, a member of the Bonaventura brigade. He settled in the Willamette Valley as a farmer. He married Margaret Bercier in 1840 and at that

[28] Francis D. Haines, Jr., "Francois Payette," *Idaho Yesterdays,* VIII (1964–65), 12–21. Professor Kenneth Holmes, Oregon College of Education, tells me he has seen the log of the *Beaver* and that Payette is mentioned in it, on one occasion as drunk.

[29] Maloney, *Bonaventura,* 102; Barker, *McLoughlin Letters,* 267.

time recognized an illegitimate son, Edward, who was, probably, the boy Work mentions as born on September 17, 1830. Pichette died on November 20, 1876, aged seventy-eight.[30]

Plante, Antoine. Company records list him as a "native." He was probably the son of Astorian Antoine Plante who disappeared from the records about 1821. His age at the time of his enlistment, his name, and the fact of his enlistment tend to support young Plante's relationship with the Astorian.

Plante first engaged with Hudson's Bay Company in 1828. For most of his career with the company, which ended in 1847, he was a trapper. Later he was employed as a *derouiner,* one who trades with the Indians where he found them or traveled with them. After he left company service, he operated a ferry on the Spokane River at the crossing of the Mullan Road. Charles Rumley, traveling from St. Louis to Portland in 1862, mentions stopping at Antoine Plante's ferry, where he bought one-half bushel of potatoes at the rate of six dollars a bushel. In the following year a newspaper report stated that "Antoine Plante—the well known half-breed, who keeps a Ferry at the crossing of the Spokane river—had found fair prospects of gold on his farm, whilst digging potatoes."[31] He died in Montana in 1890.[32]

Plante, Charles. From St. Cuthbert parish in Canada, he was born about 1790, according to Hudson's Bay Company rec-

---

[30] Maloney, *Bonaventura,* 102.

[31] Henry L. Talkington, "Mullan Road," *Washington Historical Quarterly,* VII (1916), 302; Charles Rumley, "Diary of Charles Rumley from St. Louis to Portland, 1862" (ed. by Helen A. Howard), *Sources of Northwest History,* No. 28, p. 10; *Washington Statesman* (Walla Walla), October 17, 1863. For his career with Hudson's Bay Company, see Northern Department, Abstract of Accounts, B 239/G series.

[32] LeRoy R. Hafen, ed., *The Mountain Men and the Fur Trade of the Far West,* V, 296.

ords.[33] He first enlisted in the fur trade in 1808 and joined the Northwest Company in 1811. He served in the Athabasca District until his transfer to the Columbia Department in 1814. In 1821 his name appears on the roster of men who were transferred from Northwest Company service to Hudson's Bay Company in the Columbia Department. He served with Finan MacDonald on an expedition to central Oregon in 1825–26.[34] Charles Plante was with Ogden in the expedition of 1826–27. He was also with the 1828–29 brigade and, probably, with that of 1829–30. He stayed with the brigade through the two difficult expeditions of 1831–32 and 1832–33, but he seems to have spent the following two years as a free trapper in the Willamette Valley. In 1835 he retired to become a settler and so lived out his life, dying on August 16, 1854, at the home of Charles Rondeau, one of the trappers of the 1830–31 brigade.[35]

Plante, Miquam. He was a half-blood and seems to have been brother to Antoine Plante. He was with Work again in 1831, deserting the party on October 23, 1831. He rejoined the brigade on January 20, 1832, and accompanied Dumais on the canoe trip on the Salmon River which ended in the two being drowned in July, 1832.[36]

Quintall, Laurent. He was from the parish of St. Pierre, District of Montreal. He was with Ogden in 1824–25 and was one of the few who stood by Ogden in the scuffle with the deserters

[33] Charles Plante could not have been the son of Astorian Antoine Plante despite the unsupported assertion of some historians, *e.g.*, Hafen, *ibid.*, 291. For the information on his home and approximate date of birth, see B 239/G/5, f. 39.

[34] Quebec, *Rapport de L'Archiviste . . . de Quebec . . . 1945–1946*, 275; F 4/64, 27; B 239/1/1, f. 79.

[35] *HBRS*, XXIII, 2, 7, 7n., 15, 34–35, 230; B 202/a/8; B 202/a/11, passim; Maloney, *Bonaventura*, 4, 75, 103; B 223/d/54, f. 4; B 223/d/61, f. 8; B. 223/d/77, p. 9; Nichols, *Mantle*, 305.

[36] Work, Field Journal, 1831–32, dates as given.

in May, 1825. He was with Work again in 1831–32 and with the Bonaventura brigade of 1832–33. He was married in 1839, at which time he gave his occupation as *engagé* and hunter. When his son was baptized in the following year, he gave his occupation as farmer, apparently having retired from the fur trade. He was still living as late as 1857.[37]

Rocque, George Ross dit Rocque is variously referred to as George R. Rocque and George Ross Rocque. He is not mentioned in the Work journal for 1831–32 but was with the Bonaventura expedition of 1832–33. Efforts to identify him as a Willamette settler have been in vain.[38]

Rondeau, Charles. He was thirty-seven years of age at this time and was from the parish of Sorel. This was his fifteenth year of service in the fur trade. He was with Ogden in the Snake Country as early as the brigade of 1825–26 and served continuously with the brigade through the Bonaventura expedition of Work in 1832–33. By 1836 he had retired to become a settler in the Willamette Valley. He was credited with £29 / 3s. for wheat sold at Fort Vancouver on the outfit of 1840 and was still alive in August, 1854.[39]

Rondeau, Louis. The eldest son of Joseph Rondeau of Berthier, Montreal, he entered the fur trade in 1818 and spent most of his career in the Pacific Northwest. He was an *engagé* with Ogden in 1825–26 as a freeman with that brigade. He was unable to accompany Work in 1831 because of illness and remained at Fort Nez Perces, but in January, 1832, he rejoined Work, a

---

[37] Nichols, *Mantle*, 270, 290, 328; *HBRS*, XIII, 234; Maloney, *Bonaventura*, 103, 107.

[38] Maloney, *Bonaventura*, 103, 107. In company records and accounts his name is given as George Ross *dit* Rocque. The form given above was that used by Work in this journal, hence the preference given to it in the editing.

[39] *HBRS*, XXIII, 2; B 239/1/11. f. 66; Nichols, *Mantle*, 305.

feat that shows remarkable courage. Most of the remainder of his career was spent with the Southern party as an *engagé*. He was married in October, 1842, and retired to become a Willamette settler in 1845.[40]

Sanders, John Alexander or Jean. He is not listed with any of the other Snake Country expeditions nor with the Bonaventura brigade of 1832–33. His wife died in March, 1842. When he remarried in May of that year, he listed his occupation as farmer.[41]

St. Germain, Soteaux. As the name Soteaux (also spelled Solteaux) indicates, he was a Chipewyan Indian. He had been with Finan MacDonald in 1823 and with Ross in the Snake Country in 1824, and he stayed on with Ogden in the brigade of 1824–25. He was usually a freeman, which probably accounts for the fact that his name is not listed with other Snake Country brigades though it seems certain that he was with them. He was with Work again in 1831–32 until his death in July, 1832. Work at first seems to have been of the opinion that the old man, growing senile, had lost his way and died of exposure, but he came to believe a later account that St. Germain had been murdered by the Mountain Snakes. St. Germain left a family that was cared for by the Columbia Department for many years.[42]

Tewatcon, Thomas. An Iroquois from Sault St. Louis, Canada, he was with Alexander Roderick McLeod on the 1828 expedition to recover Jedediah Smith's property. He is not men-

[40] Nichols, *Mantle*, 294; B 146/a/1, p. 21, 38; B 202/a/11, January 20, 1832; B 223/d/100, p. 9; B 239/g/25, f. 91.
[41] Nichols, *Mantle*, 292.
[42] *HBRS*, XIII, 68n, 219; Maloney, *Bonaventura*, 6. The charge for the support of the family is to be found in the annual district statements of the Columbia Department, Hudson's Bay Company Archives, B 239/L Series.

tioned in the other Snake Country journals prior to this one, nor is he mentioned in the 1831–32 journal. He was with Work again in 1832–33, and it seems probable that he had served with Work on the other expedition as well. He was married in 1839. The date of his death is uncertain, but it occurred prior to September, 1848.[43]

Toupin, Jean. He was from Mackinonge, Canada. He was first listed in the company records in the Columbia Department in 1821. In 1824 he was listed as twenty-five years old, with nine years service and serving in the grade of interpreter. As interpreter at Fort Nez Perces in 1829–30, he apparently had a falling out with the clerk in charge and left for the Snake Country with Work. He remained with the expedition in 1831–32 and again in the following year. He then returned to Fort Nez Perces as interpreter, a position he held until the summer of 1841. On July 19, 1841, he was formally married to Madame Dorion, with whom he had been living for more than ten years. The date of his death is not known, but it must have been prior to 1851, when Madame Dorion remarried.[44]

Turner, John. One of the four survivors of the Jedediah Smith party, which was massacred on the Umpqua River in 1828, he helped guide the McLeod party in 1828–29 in its attempt to recover Smith's property from the Indians. Later he guided Michel Laframboise and his party on a trapping expedition to California. After paying his debts he left the party to join Ewing Young in California in January, 1833. He seems to

[43] Nichols, *Mantle,* 269, 303; M. S. Sullivan, *The Travels of Jedediah Smith,* plate facing page 116, a reproduction of a page of the Alexander Roderick McLeod journal of the Umpqua expedition; Maloney, *Bonaventura,* 103.

[44] Nichols, *Mantle,* 290, 330; B 239/g/4, f. 43; B 239/x/2, p. 499; B 239/L/11, f. 41; B 223/g/6, f. 37; B 146/a/1, September 3, 1831; Maloney, *Bonaventura,* 101.

have settled in the Willamette Valley for a time, as his son was baptized at the Mission in 1840. At that time he was farming. He was with the second Donner relief party, and he died in California in 1847.[45]

Tyaquariche, Baptiste. An Iroquois who had served with the Northwest Company before the merger with Hudson's Bay Company, he was with Ogden in the Snake Country in 1824–25 and was one of those who deserted to the Americans under Gardiner in January, 1825. He returned to company service in time to serve with Ogden again in the expedition of 1826-27, being seriously wounded in a fray with the Indians on October 15, 1826. He became a freeman in 1827 but appears to have remained with the Snake Country brigade continuously until he deserted to the Americans again on April 16, 1831. Because he did not return to company service, his career is unknown after this.[46]

[45] Sullivan, *Travels of Jedediah Smith*, 108; Maloney, *Bonaventura*, 27, 105; Nichols, *Mantle*, 289.
Kenneth L. Holmes holds that Turner stayed with Ewing Young for several years because Turner was one of those participating in the Willamette Cattle Company. (Kenneth L. Holmes, *Ewing Young, Master Trapper*, 120.)
[46] *HBRS*, XXIII, 13 and 13n. See above, April 16, 1831.

Appendix B:

Ogden's Letter
About the Expedition's Route

Letter Number 125.[1]

FORT NES PERCY   21st August, 1830

MR JOHN WORK

SIR

You having requested my opinion relative to the route you should take in quest of Beaver as I am not authorised to give you instructions I shall merely state the track I had intended following had I returned.—From this by the usual *route* to the Snake River (S. B.) ascending this stream to *Campment Fusil* where you will cross it and proceed to Reeds River here or in the vicinity you will separate from Alex: Carson and five Men who are to remain and hunt in that quarter. The Men that are to accompany him, it is generally understood in similar cases are Volunteers so in case of being unfortunate they can attach no blame to you. The different Forking Party's that have separated from me have invariably succeeded well in returns but the reverse in regards to Horses Traps the latter how-

[1] Permission to print this valuable document in full has been granted by the owner, Mr. Burt Brown Barker of Portland, Oregon. The version which follows is that which appears in his work, *Letters of John McLoughlin*, pp. 125–28. No reproduction of this text may be made without the express written consent of Mr. Barker.

I have omitted the editor's additions from Barker's text as I did not feel that they were necessary in this work.—Editor.

154

ever must be a secondary consideration in the Snake Country, after separating from the above Party yours will be sufficiently strong to oppose the Blackfeet. Leaving Reeds River proceed across Camass Plains to Sickly River, on this stream its branches and the Swamps you will find Beaver to employ you for some time as you will not return by this *route* in the Spring and should the season be not too far advanced you might proceed by the sources of the North Branche of Sickly River to the waters of the Salmon River but should there be an appearance of an early winter I would advise you to loose sight of Salmon River and loose no time in crossing over the Plains of the *Trois Butes* (Three Knobs) to the South Branche for should you unfortunately be too late in crossing in the Fall altho the distance is only 40 miles from the depth of snow in the Spring it would be late in May ere you could cross it when you would have to contend with the floods and consequently loose your Spring Hunt., on reaching the South Branche in the Fall in selecting a place to winter in for the Safety of your Party and Horses it would be to your Interest to place yourself in such a situation that the Snake Camp be in your advance which will be a security to you against the Black Feet still your day and night watch must be most strictly attended to from the day you reach Reeds River until your return here— As soon as the navigation is free from ice ascend the South Branche as far as you find Beaver to employ you or so long as the rising of the waters do not prevent you from Trapping, on leaving the South Branche Louis Kanata [*sic*] will be able to guide you across the Country to Bears River, on this stream excepting the Lower part and a small Fork that discharges in Great Salt Lake or in a salt marsh particularly at its Sources you will find a few Beavers from thence you will proceed to Unknown River, Indians report— another river to the Southward of Unknown River, this stream I did not see but am not of opinion it can be very long otherwise in my journey last year would have discovered it, if your time permits you might easily discover if there be one or not— leaving U. River proceed across to Sandwich Island River it is formed by two principal streams the first you will find was trapp'd two years since and the other four years and it seems was never seen by me   this will conclude your hunt for from thence to F^t Nez Perce you will scarcely collect 50 beavers On leaving the Buffalo Country so thoughtless are the Canadians you cannot too often remind them of the necessity of securing a stock of Provisions for nearly two Months also the necessity while the Buffaloes are fat to make *Appichomons Parfleches & Lodges* so as to make themselves independent of any supplys at this place— The Men in general are careful of their Beaver. Still you will require to give both them and the leaders a hint occasionally by reminding the former a Shilling less will be paid for each skin and the latter their usual presents will be curtailed— Louis Kanota and Francois Payette from their knowledge of the Country will be enabled to give you any information you may require as from any other you can place little or no reliance to suit their own interest or views will assert any thing— The rules and regulations in regard to Camp are as follows— No Man exempted from going on discovery or to any place required for the general Interest— No Man exempted from night watch excepting the day Guard. No one is allowed to start before the Leader is ready and gives the *calls* the same in regard to Encamping, when ⅔ of the Trappers/have their traps in the water it is understood you remain in Camp, you will find it to your interest to select good plains for your Camp when in the Black foot Country, on Sickly River you may expect to see them. In April May, June & July you will do well to keep your Horses tied at night. the nights are then short and you ought to have from four to five Men on each Watch, when grassing in the Morning your Horses should be kept as near the Camp as you possibly can to guard against surprise for when they find they cannot succeed at night they will make an attempt in the day, permit me again to remark you cannot be too careful *all* depends on them. by keeping them so closely confined you must in consequence regulate your travelling accordingly— The Engaged Men are not entitled to any Rations from their starting from this to their Return and are obliged to supply you with food when in their power— The usual time for the Party to reach this is from the 10th to 15th July and you will require to warn Alex. Carson to be here from the 5th to the 10th it is preferrable he should be detain'd a few days waiting for you than you for him— You will find Chas. Plante, Augustin Finlay, Lo Kanota leading Men, by carefully watching their motions you can easily manage the remainders Having nothing further to remark I beg leave to offer you my best wishes for a safe and prosperous journey

I remain Dear Sir

Yrs Trly—P. S. Ogden

Bibliography

The works which have been used in editing are listed below with one exception. The unpublished documents from the Hudson's Bay Company Archives, in accord with general practice in dealing with these materials, are cited according to the Archival identification numbers in the footnotes. A listing of these numbers below would hardly be useful.

PRIMARY SOURCES

Barker, Burt Brown (ed.). *Letters of John McLoughlin Written at Fort Vancouver, 1829–1832.* Portland, 1948.

Cox, Ross. *The Columbia River.* Ed. by Edgar I. Stewart and Jane R. Stewart. Norman, Oklahoma, 1957.

Davies, K. G., and A. M. Johnson (eds.). *Peter Skene Ogden's Snake Country Journal, 1826–27.* Vol. XXIII of Hudson's Bay Record Society Series. London, 1961.

Dee, Henry Drummond (ed.). *The Journal of John Work, January to October, 1835.* Victoria, British Columbia, 1945.

Douglas, David. *Journal Kept by David Douglas, 1823–27.* London, 1914.

Elliott, T. C. (ed.). "Journal of Alexander Ross. Snake Country Expedition, 1824," *Oregon Historical Quarterly,* Vol. XIV (1913), 369–88.

———— (ed.). "Journal of John Work, April 30th to May 31st, 1830," *Oregon Historical Quarterly,* Vol. X (1909), 296–313.

———— (ed.). "Journal of John Work, Covering Snake Country

Expedition of 1830–31," *Oregon Historical Quarterly,* Vol. XIII (1912), 363–71; Vol. XIV (1913), 281–314.

————— (ed.). "Journal of John Work, November and December, 1824," *Washington Historical Quarterly,* Vol. III (1912), 200.

————— (ed.). "Journal of Peter Skene Ogden; Snake Expedition, 1827–28," *Oregon Historical Quarterly,* Vol. XI (1910), 361–79.

————— (ed.). "Journal of Peter Skene Ogden; Snake Expedition, 1828–29," *Oregon Historical Quarterly,* Vol. XI (1910), 381–96.

Ferris, Warren Angus. *Life in the Rocky Mountains.* Ed. by J. Cecil Alter. Salt Lake City, ca. 1940.

Franchère, Gabriel. *Adventure at Astoria, 1810–1814.* Trans. and ed. by Hoyt C. Franchère. Norman, Oklahoma, 1967.

Frémont, John Charles. *Narratives of Exploration and Adventure.* Ed. by Allen Nevins. New York, 1956.

Hudson's Bay Record Series. *The Letters of John McLoughlin from Fort Vancouver to the Governor and Committee,* 1st–3rd Series. See E. E. Rich (ed.).

—————. *Minutes of the Council Northern Department of Rupert Land, 1821–31.* See E. E. Rich (ed.).

—————. *Part of Dispatch from George Simpson, Esqr.* See E. E. Rich (ed.).

—————. *Peter Skene Ogden's Snake Country Journal, 1826–27.* See K. G. Davies and A. M. Johnson (eds.).

—————. *Peter Skene Ogden's Snake Country Journals, 1824–25 and 1825–26.* See E. E. Rich (ed.).

McLoughlin, John. *Letters from Fort Vancouver to the Governor and Committee, First Series, 1825–38.* See E. E. Rich (ed.).

—————. *Letters from Fort Vancouver to the Governor and Committee, Second Series, 1839–44.* See E. E. Rich (ed.).

—————. *Letters from Fort Vancouver to the Governor and Committee, Third Series, 1844–46.* See E. E. Rich (ed.).

—————. *Letters Written at Fort Vancouver, 1829–32.* See Burt Brown Barker (ed.).

Maloney, Alice Bay (ed.). *Fur Brigade to Bonaventura. John*

Work's California Expedition, 1832–1833, for the Hudson's Bay Company. San Francisco, 1945.

Merk, Frederick. *Fur Trade and Empire. George Simpson's Journal, 1824–1825.* Cambridge, Massachusetts, 1931.

Ogden, Peter Skene. "Journal, Snake Expedition, 1827–28." See T. C. Elliott (ed.).

―――. "Journal, Snake Expedition, 1828–29." See T. C. Elliott (ed.).

―――. *Snake Country Journal, 1826–27.* See K. G. Davies and A. M. Johnson (eds.).

―――. *Snake Country Journals, 1824–25 and 1825–26.* See E. E. Rich (ed.).

Quaife, Milo M. (ed.). *Adventures of the First Settlers on the Oregon or Columbia River,* by Alexander Ross. Chicago, 1923.

――― (ed.). *The Fur Hunters of the Far West,* by Alexander Ross. Vol. I of the original edition. Chicago, 1924.

Quebec. *Rapport de L'Archiviste de la Province de Quebec pour 1945–1946.* Quebec, 1946.

Rich, E. E. (ed.). *The Letters of John McLoughlin from Fort Vancouver to the Governor and Committee, First Series, 1825–1838.* Vol. IV of Hudson's Bay Record Society Series. London, 1941.

――― (ed.). *The Letters of John McLoughlin from Fort Vancouver to the Governor and Committee, Third Series, 1844–46.* Vol. VI of Hudson's Bay Record Society Series. London, 1943.

――― (ed.). *The Letters of John McLoughlin from Fort Vancouver to the Governor and Committee, Third Series, 1844–46.* Vol. VII of Hudson's Bay Record Series. London, 1944.

――― (ed.). *Minutes of the Council of the Northern Department of Rupert Land, 1821–31.* Vol. III of Hudson's Bay Company Record Society Series. London, 1940.

――― (ed.). *Part of Dispatch from George Simpson, Esqr., Governor of Rupert's Land to the Governor & Committee of the Hudson's Bay Company, London.* Vol. X of Hudson's Bay Record Society Series. London, 1947.

――― (ed.). *Peter Skene Ogden's Snake Country Journals,*

1824–25 and 1825–26. Vol. XIII of Hudson's Bay Record Society Series. London, 1950.

Rollins, Philip Ashton (ed.). *The Discovery of the Oregon Trail. Robert Stuart's Narrative of His Overland Trip Eastward from Astoria in 1812–13.* New York, 1935.

Ross, Alexander. *Adventures of the First Settlers on the Oregon or Columbia River.* See Milo M. Quaife (ed.).

———. *The Fur Hunters of the Far West,* I. See Milo M. Quaife (ed.).

———. *The Fur Hunters of the Far West,* II. London, 1855.

———— "Journal, 1824." See T. C. Elliott (ed.).

Rumley, Charles. "Diary of Charles Rumley from St. Louis to Portland, 1862," ed. by Helen A. Howard. *Sources of Northwest History,* No. 28. Missoula, Montana, 1939.

Scaglione, John. "Ogden's Report of His 1829–1830 Expedition," *California Historical Society Quarterly,* Vol. XXVIII (1949), 117–24.

Simpson, George. *Part of Dispatch.* See E. E. Rich (ed.).

Stuart, Robert. *The Discovery of the Oregon Trail.* See Philip Ashton Rollins (ed.).

Sullivan, Maurice S. *The Travels of Jedediah Smith.* Santa Ana, California, 1934.

Washington Statesman (Walla Walla). October 17, 1863.

Work, John. Field Journal, 1831–32, Provincial Archives, Victoria, British Columbia.

———. "Journal, 1830." See T. C. Elliott (ed.).

———. "Journal, 1830–31." See T. C. Elliott (ed.).

———. *Journal, 1835.* See Henry Drummond Dee (ed.).

———. "Letter, 6 September 1831, Fort Nez Perces," *Washington Historical Quarterly,* Vol. I (1910), 263–64.

SECONDARY WORKS

Bancroft, Hubert Howe. *The History of Washington, Idaho, and Montana, 1845–1889.* Vol. XXXI of *The Works of Hubert Howe Bancroft.* San Francisco, 1890.

Burpee, Isaac. "The Story of John Work of the Hudson's Bay Company, June 15, 1814 to December 22nd, 1861." Bound manuscript, Provincial Archives, Victoria, British Columbia.

Chittenden, Hiram M. *The American Fur Trade of the Far West.* 2 vols. New York, ca. 1935.

Davidson, Gordon C. *The Northwest Company.* Vol. VII of *University of California Publications in History.* Berkeley, 1918.

Dee, Henry Drummond. "An Irishman in the Fur Trade: The Life and Journals of John Work," *British Columbia Historical Quarterly,* Vol. VII (1943), 229–70.

———. "John Work: A Chronicle of His Life and a Digest of His Journals." Bound manuscript, Provincial Archives, Victoria, British Columbia.

Hafen, LeRoy R. (ed.). *The Mountain Men and the Fur Trade of the Far West.* Vol. V. Glendale, California, 1968.

Haines, Francis. "McKenzie's Winter Camp," *Oregon Historical Quarterly,* Vol. XXXVII (1936), 329–33.

———. *Red Eagles of the Northwest.* Portland, 1939.

Haines, Francis D., Jr. "Death of a Snake Country Trapper: Pierre L'Etang," *Oregon Historical Quarterly,* Vol. LVI, (1955), 248–54.

———. "Francois Payette," *Idaho Yesterdays,* Vol. VIII (1964–65), 12–21.

———. "The Lost River of John Day," *Idaho Yesterdays,* Vol. II (1969), 6–10.

Holmes, Kenneth L. *Ewing Young, Master Trapper.* Portland, 1967.

Madsen, Brigham D. *The Bannock of Idaho.* Caldwell, Idaho, 1958.

Maloney, Alice Bay. "Alexander Carson, Wilhamot Freeman," *Oregon Historical Quarterly,* Vol. XXXIX (1938), 16–21.

Nichols, M. Leona. *The Mantle of Elias.* Portland, 1941.

Porter, Kenneth Wiggins. "Roll of the Overland Astorians, 1810–12," *Oregon Historical Quarterly,* Vol. XXXIV (1933), 103–12.

Sage, Walter N. *Sir James Douglas and British Columbia.* Toronto, 1930.

Schultz, James Willard. *With the Indians in the Rockies.* Cambridge, Massachusetts, 1925.

Talkington, Henry L. "Mullan Road," *Washington Historical Quarterly*, Vol. VII (1916), 301–306.

Wissler, Clark. *Indians of the United States.* New York, 1940.

Index

THE AMERICAN EXPLORATION AND TRAVEL SERIES
follows rather logically the University of Oklahoma Press's pro-
gram of regional exploration, with fifty-nine volumes portraying
the story of the gradual and inevitable recession of the American
frontier published since the series was announced in 1938. Volumes
in print in this series:

1. *Adventure on Red River: Report on the Exploration of the
   Headwaters of the Red River*, by Captain Randolph B. Marcy
   and Captain G. B. McClellan, ed. by Grant Foreman. $4.50.
2. *Marcy and the Gold Seekers: The Journal of Captain R. B.
   Marcy, with an Account of the Gold Rush over the Southern
   Route*, by Grant Foreman. $6.95.
3. *Tabeau's Narrative of Loisel's Expedition to the Upper Missouri*, ed. by Annie Heloise Abel, trans. by Rose Abel Wright.
   $6.50.
4. *Tixier's Travels on the Osage Prairies*, ed. by John Francis
   McDermott, trans. by Albert J. Salvan. $7.50.
5. *Teodoro de Croix and the Northern Frontier of New Spain,
   1776–1783*, trans. and ed. by Alfred Barnaby Thomas. $5.95.
6. *A Pathfinder in the Southwest: The Itinerary of Lieutenant
   A. W. Whipple During His Explorations for a Railway Route
   from Fort Smith to Los Angeles in the Years 1851 & 1854*,
   ed. by Grant Foreman. $7.50.
8. *The Western Journals of Washington Irving*, ed. by John
   Francis McDermott. $7.50.
10. *Maya Explorer: John Lloyd Stephens and the Lost Cities of
    Central America and Yucatán*, by Victor Wolfgang von
    Hagen. $6.95.
12. *The Lost Pathfinder: Zebulon Montgomery Pike*, by W.
    Eugene Hollon. $4.50.
17. *Commerce of the Prairies*, by Josiah Gregg, ed. by Max L.
    Moorhead. $8.50.
18. *Indian Sketches, Taken During an Expedition to the Pawnee*

Tribes [1833], by John Treat Irving, Jr., ed. by John Francis McDermott. $7.50.

19. *Travels in the Old South: 1527–1825: A Bibliography*, ed. by Thomas D. Clark. Volume One, *The Formative Years, 1527–1783: From the Spanish Explorations through the American Revolution.* Volume Two, *The Expanding South, 1750–1825: The Ohio Valley and the Cotton Frontier.* Volume Three, *The Ante Bellum South, 1825–1860: Cotton, Slavery, and Conflict.* Three volumes, boxed. $45.00.

20. *The Fur Hunters of the Far West*, by Alexander Ross, ed. by Kenneth A. Spaulding. $6.95.

22. *Joseph Reddeford Walker and the Arizona Adventure*, by David Ellis Conner, ed. by Donald J. Berthrong and Odessa Davenport. $7.50.

23. *Prairie and Mountain Sketches*, by Matthew C. Field, collected by Clyde and Mae Reed Porter, ed. by Kate L. Gregg and John Francis McDermott. $6.95.

24. *The Columbia River*, by Ross Cox, ed. by Edgar I. and Jane R. Stewart. $7.95.

25. *The Texan-Santa Fé Pioneers*, by Noel Loomis. $6.95.

27. *Journey Through the Rocky Mountains and the Humboldt Mountains to the Pacific Ocean*, by Jacob H. Schiel, trans. and ed. by Thomas N. Bonner. $5.95.

28. *Adventures of Zenas Leonard, Fur Trader*, ed. by John C. Ewers. $5.95.

29. *Matt Field on the Santa Fe Trail*, collected by Clyde and Mae Reed Porter, ed. and introduction by John Sunder. $7.50.

30. *The Road to Virginia City: The Diary of James Knox Polk Miller*, ed. by Andrew F. Rolle. $5.95.

31. *The Gila Trail: The Texas Argonauts and the California Gold Rush*, by Benjamin Butler Harris, ed. by Richard H. Dillon. $5.95.

33. *From St. Louis to Sutter's Fort, 1846*, by Heinrich Lienhard, trans. and ed. by Erwin G. and Elisabeth K. Gudde. $5.95.

34. *The Adventures of Captain Bonneville, U.S.A., in the Rocky*

Mountains and the Far West, digested from the journal by Washington Irving, ed. and introduction by Edgeley W. Todd. $9.95.

35. *Jean-Bernard Bossu's Travels in the Interior of North America, 1751–1762,* by Jean-Bernard Bossu, trans. and ed. by Seymour Feiler. $6.95.

36. *Travels in the New South: 1865–1955: A Bibliography,* ed. by Thomas D. Clark. Volume One, *The Postwar South, 1865–1900.* Volume Two, *The Twentieth-Century South, 1900–1955.* The set $20.00. (See volume 19).

37. *Incidents of Travel in Yucatán,* by John Lloyd Stephens, ed. and introduction by Victor Wolfgang von Hagen. 2 vols. $24.95.

38. *Great Surveys of the American West,* by Richard A. Bartlett. $8.95.

40. *The New Democracy in America: The Travels of Francisco de Miranda in the United States, 1783–84,* trans. by Judson P. Wood, ed. by John S. Ezell. $6.50.

41. *Mansfield on the Condition of the Western Forts, 1853–54,* ed. by Robert W. Frazer. $6.95.

42. *Adventure in the Wilderness: The American Journals of Louis Antoine de Bougainville, 1756–1760,* trans. and ed. by Edward P. Hamilton. $7.95.

43. *Navaho Expedition: Journal of a Military Reconnaissance from Santa Fe, New Mexico, to the Navaho Country, Made in 1849,* by James H. Simpson, ed. by Frank McNitt. $7.50.

44. *Astoria; or, Anecdotes of an Enterprise Beyond the Rocky Mountains,* by Washington Irving, ed. and introduction by Edgeley W. Todd. $12.50.

45. *Down the Colorado,* by Robert Brewster Stanton, ed. by Dwight L. Smith. $6.95.

46. *My Life in the Mountains and on the Plains: The Newly Discovered Autobiography,* by David Meriwether, ed. by Robert A. Griffen. $6.95.

47. *The Valley of the Upper Yellowstone,* by Charles W. Cook,

David E. Folsom, and William Peterson, ed. and introduction by Aubrey L. Haines. $5.95.

48. *The Journals and Papers of Zebulon Montgomery Pike*, ed. by Donald Jackson, 2 vols. $20.00.

49. *Pedro Vial and the Roads to Santa Fe*, by Noel M. Loomis and Abraham P. Nasatir. $12.50.

50. *Exploring the Northwest Territory: Sir Alexander Mackenzie's Journal of a Voyage by Bark Canoe from Lake Athabasca to the Pacific Ocean in the Summer of 1789*, ed. by T. H. McDonald. $4.95.

51. *The Original Journals of Henry Smith Turner: With Stephen Watts Kearny to New Mexico and California, 1846*, ed. by Dwight L. Clarke. $5.95.

52. *Palenque: The Walker-Caddy Expedition to the Ancient Maya City, 1839–1840*, by David M. Pendergast. $6.95.

54. *On the Western Tour with Washington Irving: The Journal and Letters of Count de Pourtalès*, trans. by Seymour Feiler, ed. and introduction by George F. Spaulding. $5.95.

55. *For Science and National Glory: The Spanish Scientific Expedition to America, 1862–1866*, by Robert Ryal Miller. $5.95.

56. *The Missouri Expedition of 1818–1820: The Journal of Surgeon John Gale*, ed. by Roger L. Nichols. $5.95.

57. *The California Coast: Documents from the Sutro Collection*, ed. and introduction by Donald C. Cutter. $7.50.

58. *Thomas Gage's Travels in the New World*, ed. and introduction by J. Eric S. Thompson. $8.95.

59. *The Snake Country Expedition of 1830–31: John Work's Field Journal*, ed. and introduction by Francis D. Haines, Jr. $7.95.